D1317092

Microsoft® Office
PowerPoint®
2010: Part 1

Microsoft® Office PowerPoint® 2010: Part 1

Part Number: 091031
Course Edition: 2.2

Acknowledgements

PROJECT TEAM

Author	Media Designer	Content Editor
Tim Barnosky	Alex Tong	Catherine M. Albano

Notices

DISCLAIMER

While Logical Operations, Inc. takes care to ensure the accuracy and quality of these materials, we cannot guarantee their accuracy, and all materials are provided without any warranty whatsoever, including, but not limited to, the implied warranties of merchantability or fitness for a particular purpose. The name used in the data files for this course is that of a fictitious company. Any resemblance to current or future companies is purely coincidental. We do not believe we have used anyone's name in creating this course, but if we have, please notify us and we will change the name in the next revision of the course. Logical Operations is an independent provider of integrated training solutions for individuals, businesses, educational institutions, and government agencies. Use of screenshots, photographs of another entity's products, or another entity's product name or service in this book is for editorial purposes only. No such use should be construed to imply sponsorship or endorsement of the book by, nor any affiliation of such entity with Logical Operations. This courseware may contain links to sites on the internet that are owned and operated by third parties (the "External Sites"). Logical Operations is not responsible for the availability of, or the content located on or through, any External Site. Please contact Logical Operations if you have any concerns regarding such links or External Sites.

TRADEMARK NOTICES

Logical Operations and the Logical Operations logo are trademarks of Logical Operations, Inc. and its affiliates.

Microsoft® Office PowerPoint® 2010 is a registered trademark of Microsoft Corporation in the U.S. and other countries. The other Microsoft products and services discussed or described may be trademarks or registered trademarks of Microsoft Corporation. All other product and service names used may be common law or registered trademarks of their respective proprietors.

Copyright © 2013 Logical Operations, Inc. All rights reserved. Screenshots used for illustrative purposes are the property of the software proprietor. This publication, or any part thereof, may not be reproduced or transmitted in any form or by any means, electronic or mechanical, including photocopying, recording, storage in an information retrieval system, or otherwise, without express written permission of Logical Operations, 3535 Winton Place, Rochester, NY 14623, 1-800-456-4677 in the United States and Canada, 1-585-350-7000 in all other countries. Logical Operations' World Wide Web site is located at **www.logicaloperations.com.**

This book conveys no rights in the software or other products about which it was written; all use or licensing of such software or other products is the responsibility of the user according to terms and conditions of the owner. Do not make illegal copies of books or software. If you believe that this book, related materials, or any other Logical Operations materials are being reproduced or transmitted without permission, please call 1-800-456-4677 in the United States and Canada, 1-585-350-7000 in all other countries.

Microsoft® Office PowerPoint® 2010: Part 1

About This Course

It's hard to imagine a day going by without people passing along large amounts of information. Messages are everywhere, and the number of messages we receive seems to be increasing each day. Whether via phone, email, mass media, or personal interaction, we are subjected to a constant stream of information. With so much communication to contend with, it can be difficult to grab people's attention. But, we are often called upon to do just that. So, how do you grab and maintain an audience's focus when you're asked to present important information? By being clear, organized, and engaging. And, that is exactly what Microsoft® Office PowerPoint® 2010 can help you do.

Gone are the days of flip charts or drawing on a white board to illustrate your point. Today's audiences are tech savvy, accustomed to high-impact multimedia content, and stretched for time. By learning how to use the vast array of features and functionality contained within PowerPoint 2010, you will gain the ability to organize your content, enhance it with high-impact visuals, and deliver it with a punch. In this course, you will use PowerPoint 2010 to begin creating engaging, dynamic multimedia presentations.

You can also use this course to prepare for the Microsoft Office Specialist (MOS) Certification exams for Microsoft PowerPoint 2010.

Course Description

Target Student

This course is designed for students who wish to gain the foundational understanding of Microsoft Office PowerPoint 2010 that is necessary to create and develop engaging multimedia presentations.

Course Prerequisites

To ensure success, students should be familiar with using personal computers, and should have experience using a keyboard and mouse. Students should be comfortable in the Windows® 7 environment, and be able to use Windows 7 to manage information on their computers. Specific tasks the students should be able to perform include: launching and closing applications, navigating basic file structures, and managing files and folders. To meet this prerequisite, you can take any one or more of the following Logical Operations courses:

- *Microsoft® Windows® 7: Level 1*
- *Introduction to Personal Computers Using Windows® 7*

Course Objectives

Upon completing this course, you will be able to create and deliver engaging multimedia presentations that convey the key points of your message through the use of text, graphics, and animations.

You will:

- Identify the basic features and functions of PowerPoint 2010.
- Develop a PowerPoint presentation.
- Perform advanced text editing.
- Add graphical elements to a presentation.
- Modify objects in a presentation.
- Add tables to a presentation.
- Add charts to a presentation.
- Prepare to deliver a presentation.

The LogicalCHOICE Home Screen

http://www.lo-choice.com

The LogicalCHOICE Home screen is your entry point to the LogicalCHOICE learning experience, of which this course manual is only one part. Visit the LogicalCHOICE Course screen both during and after class to make use of the world of support and instructional resources that make up the LogicalCHOICE experience.

Log-on and access information for your LogicalCHOICE environment will be provided with your class experience. On the LogicalCHOICE Home screen, you can access the LogicalCHOICE Course screens for your specific courses.

Each LogicalCHOICE Course screen will give you access to the following resources:

- eBook: an interactive electronic version of the printed book for your course.
- LearnTOs: brief animated components that enhance and extend the classroom learning experience.

Depending on the nature of your course and the choices of your learning provider, the LogicalCHOICE Course screen may also include access to elements such as:

- The interactive eBook.
- Social media resources that enable you to collaborate with others in the learning community using professional communications sites such as LinkedIn or microblogging tools such as Twitter.
- Checklists with useful post-class reference information.
- Any course files you will download.
- The course assessment.
- Notices from the LogicalCHOICE administrator.
- Virtual labs, for remote access to the technical environment for your course.
- Your personal whiteboard for sketches and notes.
- Newsletters and other communications from your learning provider.
- Mentoring services.
- A link to the website of your training provider.
- The LogicalCHOICE store.

Visit your LogicalCHOICE Home screen often to connect, communicate, and extend your learning experience!

How to Use This Book

As You Learn

This book is divided into lessons and topics, covering a subject or a set of related subjects. In most cases, lessons are arranged in order of increasing proficiency.

The results-oriented topics include relevant and supporting information you need to master the content. Each topic has various types of activities designed to enable you to practice the guidelines and procedures as well as to solidify your understanding of the informational material presented in the course. Procedures and guidelines are presented in a concise fashion along with activities and discussions. Information is provided for reference and reflection in such a way as to facilitate understanding and practice.

Data files for various activities as well as other supporting files for the course are available by download from the LogicalCHOICE Course screen. In addition to sample data for the course exercises, the course files may contain media components to enhance your learning and additional reference materials for use both during and after the course.

At the back of the book, you will find a glossary of the definitions of the terms and concepts used throughout the course. You will also find an index to assist in locating information within the instructional components of the book.

As You Review

Any method of instruction is only as effective as the time and effort you, the student, are willing to invest in it. In addition, some of the information that you learn in class may not be important to you immediately, but it may become important later. For this reason, we encourage you to spend some time reviewing the content of the course after your time in the classroom.

As a Reference

The organization and layout of this book make it an easy-to-use resource for future reference. Taking advantage of the glossary, index, and table of contents, you can use this book as a first source of definitions, background information, and summaries.

Course Icons

Watch throughout the material for these visual cues:

Icon	Description
	A **Note** provides additional information, guidance, or hints about a topic or task.
	A **Caution** helps make you aware of places where you need to be particularly careful with your actions, settings, or decisions so that you can be sure to get the desired results of an activity or task.
	LearnTO notes show you where an associated LearnTO is particularly relevant to the content. Access LearnTOs from your LogicalCHOICE Course screen.
	Checklists provide job aids you can use after class as a reference to performing skills back on the job. Access checklists from your LogicalCHOICE Course screen.
	Social notes remind you to check your LogicalCHOICE Course screen for opportunities to interact with the LogicalCHOICE community using social media.
	Notes Pages are intentionally left blank for you to write on.

1 | Getting Started with PowerPoint

Lesson Time: 50 minutes

Lesson Objectives

In this lesson, you will identify the basic features and functions of Microsoft® Office PowerPoint® 2010. You will:

- Navigate the PowerPoint environment.

- Create and save a PowerPoint presentation.

- Use PowerPoint Help.

Lesson Introduction

So, you have the next great idea, and you want to pitch that idea to company leadership or to a potential client. Or, perhaps you've been called upon to present at an important function or an upcoming meeting. Regardless of the reason, you will need to express your thoughts clearly and deliver a presentation that will excite and engage your audience. You want to deliver a multimedia experience that your audience will remember.

PowerPoint 2010 can help you organize and refine your message, and to deliver your presentation with style. But, you need to be familiar with how PowerPoint works before you can take advantage of its many features. You will need to know how to find what you're looking for, how to perform the basic tasks, and how to find the help you need if you get stuck along the way. That's what you'll do in this lesson.

TOPIC A

Navigate the PowerPoint Environment

PowerPoint 2010 gives you the power and the flexibility to create an incredible array of presentations. The multimedia capabilities contained in PowerPoint allow you to add sizzle to your presentations with graphics, animation, audio, video, and a host of styles and themes. But, with so many capabilities, the task of learning how to use all of PowerPoint's features can seem daunting. So, where do you begin?

To effectively use PowerPoint's many features, you must first be able to navigate your way around the user interface. Exploring the user interface and becoming familiar with the elements of PowerPoint 2010 will start you down the path to creating engaging, professional multimedia presentations.

What Is PowerPoint?

Microsoft PowerPoint 2010 is an application that is part of the Microsoft Office 2010 suite of user productivity tools. You can use PowerPoint to create, edit, and display professional-looking graphical presentations. PowerPoint presentations contain a series of slides that are used to present graphical and textual information in a logical sequence to audiences. To increase the impact of your presentations, you can add dynamic multimedia elements that engage the audience and can enhance your credibility as a presenter.

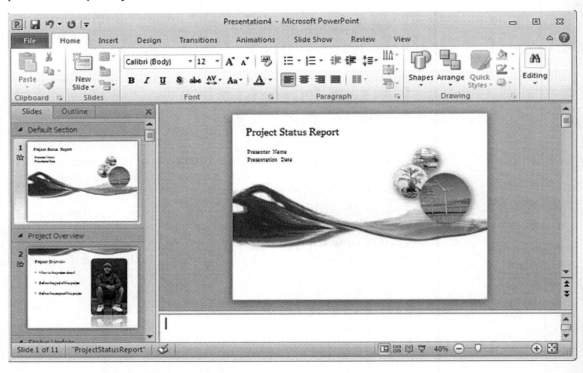

Figure 1–1: Microsoft Office PowerPoint 2010.

Slides

Slides are individual presentation objects that are used to display content to the audience. You can think of slides as being like individual pages of your presentation. You can use slides to display text, images, animations, charts, tables, video, and audio in your presentations.

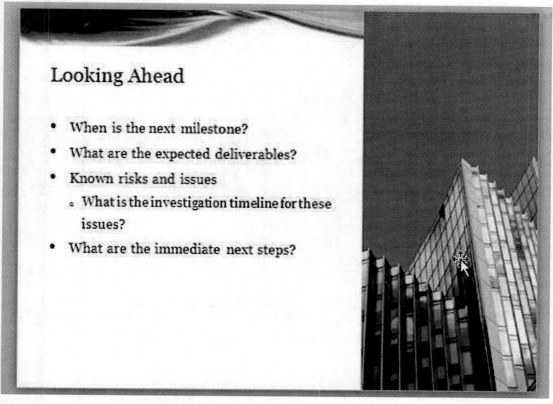

Figure 1–2: A slide in PowerPoint.

The PowerPoint 2010 Window

The PowerPoint 2010 window displays the key interface elements you will use to create and develop your presentations.

 Note: Elements of the PowerPoint 2010 user interface may appear differently, particularly the ribbon, if you display the PowerPoint window in any state other than fully maximized.

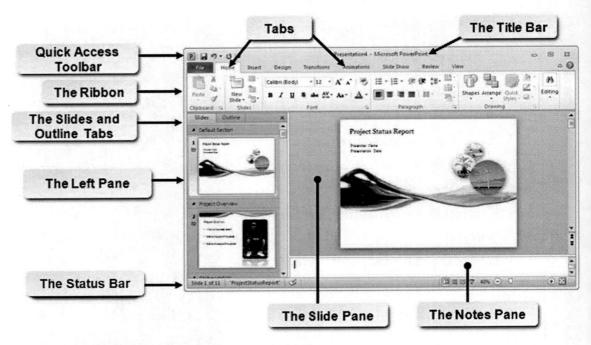

Figure 1-3: The default window in PowerPoint 2010.

The Ribbon

The *ribbon* is where you will access a majority of the commands you will use to create and develop your presentation. The ribbon is a component of the PowerPoint 2010 user interface that contains task-specific command buttons and menus grouped together under a set of tabs. The ribbon was designed to provide you with a central location for accessing the various functions of PowerPoint without having to navigate the user interface extensively.

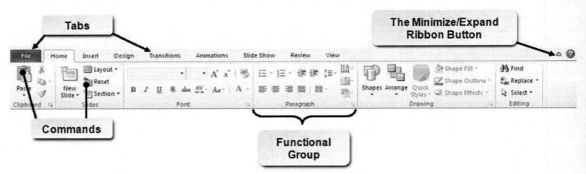

Figure 1-4: The ribbon.

Each tab contains a series of functional groups that allow you to perform related tasks.

Ribbon Tab	General Functions
File	Various commands, mainly related to manging files. Within the **File** tab, you can create, open, save, close, and print files. You can also perform other tasks, such as changing application settings.
Home	The most commonly used tasks for developing your presentation. Within the **Home** tab, you can add and edit text, add slides, and insert basic visual objects.
Insert	Options for adding and working with a variety of objects, such as charts, tables, and images.

Ribbon Tab	General Functions
Design	Options for tailoring the overall visual feel of your presentation.
Transitions	Options for creating visually appealing transitions between slides in your presentation.
Animations	Commands to add and edit animated effects in your presentation.
Slide Show	The functions you will use to deliver your final presentation.
Review	Options for reviewing and revising the various content in your presentation.
View	Commands that allow you alter how you view your presentation.

 Note: To further explore the ribbon, you can access the LearnTO **Navigate the Office 2010 Ribbon** presentation from the **LearnTO** tile on the LogicalCHOICE Course screen.

Minimize and Expand the Ribbon

You can minimize the ribbon by selecting the **Minimize the Ribbon** button. Select the same button, which becomes the **Expand the Ribbon** button when the ribbon is minimized, to expand the ribbon. Alternately, you can toggle between an expanded or a minimized ribbon by double-clicking any active tab or by pressing **Ctrl+F1**.

Screen Tips

When you hover the mouse pointer over a command or a button, a screen tip may display. Screen tips display the command name or style option, and may include a brief description of commands.

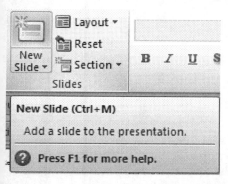

Figure 1–5: Screen tips display when you hover the mouse pointer over commands.

Key Tips

You might prefer to use keyboard shortcuts to perform the various tasks within PowerPoint. To view the key tips, which display the corresponding keyboard shortcuts for various commands, press the **Alt** key. Pressing **Alt** again will hide the key tips.

Dialog Box Launchers

Dialog box launchers are the small buttons with downward-facing arrows on the bottom-right corner of some functional groups. The dialog box launcher opens a dialog box that contains additional commands specific to the functional group. These commands allow you to perform more advanced functions not directly available on the ribbon. Dialog box launchers are active only when an appropriate slide item is selected. Otherwise, they remain grayed-out.

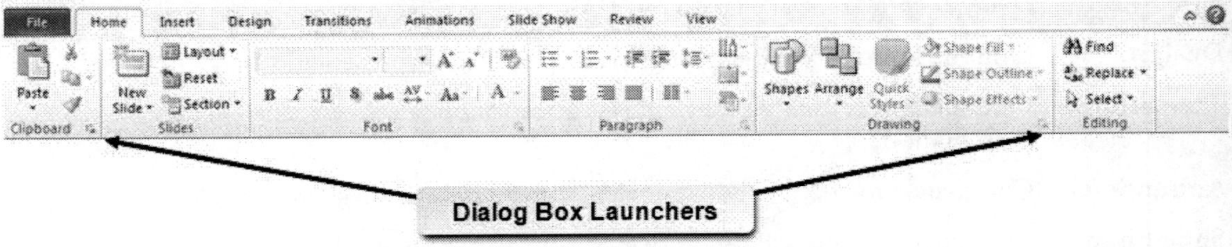

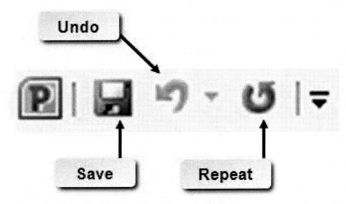

Figure 1-6: Dialog box launchers.

The Quick Access Toolbar

The *Quick Access Toolbar* provides you with easy access to some of the most commonly used commands within PowerPoint. By default, the **Quick Access Toolbar** displays the **Save**, **Undo**, and **Repeat** buttons. You can customize the **Quick Access Toolbar** to include other commands that you frequently use.

Figure 1-7: The Quick Access Toolbar.

The Slides Tab

The *Slides tab* displays in the left pane of the PowerPoint 2010 user interface by default. All of the slides in your presentation are displayed in the **Slides** tab as thumbnails. You can navigate through the slides in your presentation by selecting the thumbnails in the **Slides** tab, or by pressing the **Up Arrow** and **Down Arrow** keys.

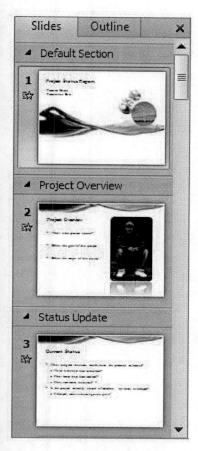

Figure 1-8: Use the Slides tab to navigate the slides in your presentation.

The Outline Tab

The *Outline tab* is an optional view of the slides in your presentation available in the left pane. The **Outline** tab displays the slides in outline form, showing the titles, the subtitles, and the text from your slides. In the **Outline** tab, the slides are not displayed as thumbnails. You can switch from the default Slides tab view to the **Outline** tab view by selecting the **Outline** tab.

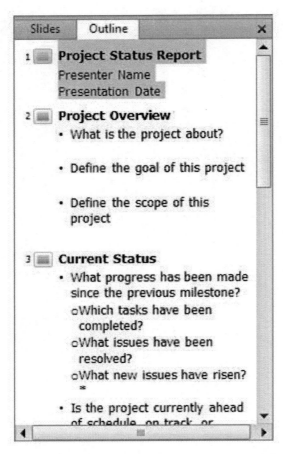

Figure 1-9: The Outline tab displays your slides in outline form.

 Note: You can edit the text on your slides in the Outline view. Editing text will be covered in further detail in Lessons 2 and 3.

The Status Bar

The *status bar* is located across the bottom of the PowerPoint window. It displays information about the currently selected slide and provides you with quick access to some of the basic view options.

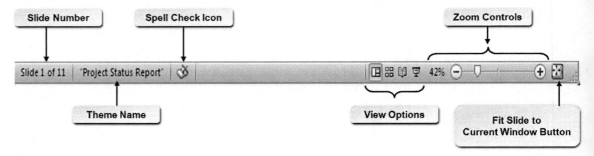

Figure 1-10: The status bar.

Status Bar Element	Description
Slide Number	Displays the currently selected slide number and the total number of slides in your presentation.

Status Bar Element	Description
Theme Name	Displays the name of the theme applied to the currently selected slide.
Spell Check icon	The **Spell Check** icon is displayed with a red check mark if there are spelling errors in your presentation. You can select the icon to resolve the spelling errors.
View options	Allow you to select from among the following view options: **Normal, Slide Sorter, Reading**, and **Slide Show**.
Zoom controls	Allow you to select your desired zoom level and displays the zoom percentage.
Fit Slide to Current Window button	Displays the slide at the ideal zoom level for the current PowerPoint window.

Contextual Tabs

Contextual tabs are highly specialized tabs that appear on the ribbon when certain objects are selected. Contextual tabs contain specific commands and menus related to items such as tables, charts, and pictures. You can edit the particular attributes of these items within their respective contextual tabs. Some contextual tabs contain multiple tabs for accessing commands. Once the item is deselected, the contextual tab will disappear.

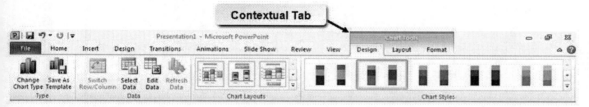

Figure 1–11: The Chart Tools contextual tab contains multiple tabs.

The Backstage View

The *Backstage view* appears on the PowerPoint user interface when you select the **File** tab. The **Backstage** view contains vertically aligned tabs that give you access to groups of related commands and options. These commands and options allow you to perform many of the tasks associated with managing files and configuring application settings.

You can think of the **Backstage** view as where you go to do things to files. Whereas, the other ribbon tabs are where you go to do things within files.

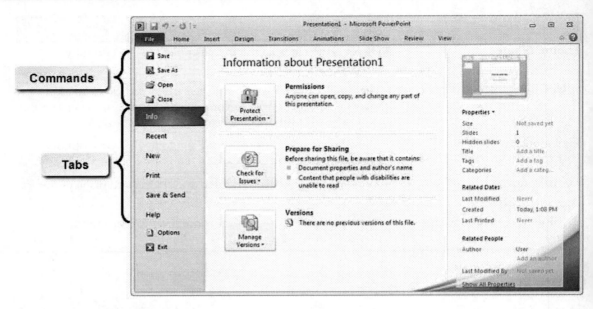

Figure 1-12: The Backstage view.

ACTIVITY 1-1
Navigating the PowerPoint 2010 User Interface

Scenario

You are the newest product design engineer for Develetech Industries, a manufacturer of home electronics. Develetech is known as an innovative designer and producer of high-end televisions, video game consoles, laptop and tablet computers, and mobile phones.

Develetech is a mid-sized company, employing approximately 2,000 residents of Greene City and the surrounding area. Develetech also contracts with a number of offshore organizations for manufacturing and supply-chain support.

You have been hired as part of the new product development team. You will play an active role in the research, design, and prototyping of new Develetech products. You have expertise in electrical engineering as well as product and visual design. Additionally, you have experience managing teams of undergraduate and graduate students for major university research and design projects.

As part of Develetech's new product development team, you know you will be asked to create presentations to pitch new product ideas to your team and to company management. In your previous experience, you used a number of applications for the delivery of multimedia presentations, but never PowerPoint. Develetech Industries uses PowerPoint 2010 to create all multimedia presentations, so you realize you will need to learn how to use it. You decide the best way to start is by exploring the PowerPoint user interface.

---

1. Launch PowerPoint 2010.
   a) Select the **Start** menu from the Windows desktop.
   b) Select **All Programs→Microsoft Office→Microsoft PowerPoint 2010**.

2. Explore the PowerPoint 2010 interface by identifying the following elements: the **Slide** pane, the **Notes** pane, the **Slides** tab, the **Outline** tab, the **Quick Access Toolbar**, the tabs, the ribbon, the title bar, and the status bar.

3. Explore the ribbon.
   a) Select various ribbon tabs.
   b) Observe the functional groups changing as you select the various tabs.
   c) Select the **Design** tab and, in the **Background** group, select the **dialog box launcher**.
   d) Observe that the **Format Background** dialog box has launched.
   e) Close the **Format Background** dialog box.
   f) Select the **Insert** tab.
   g) In the **Illustrations** group, hover the mouse pointer over the **Shapes** button to view its screen tip.
   h) Select the **Minimize the Ribbon** button to hide the ribbon. Select it again to restore the ribbon.

4. Explore the **Backstage** view.
   a) Select the **File** tab.
   b) Observe that the **Save**, **Save As**, **Open**, and **Close** commands appear above the **Backstage View** tabs.
   c) Select the **New** tab, and then select the **Print** tab.
   d) Observe that the available options change as you navigate the **Backstage View** tabs.
   e) Select the **File** tab again to close the **Backstage View** and return to the previously selected ribbon tab.

5. Explore the **Quick Access Toolbar**.

   a) Hover the mouse pointer over the **Save** button to view its tool tip.

   b) Select the **Customize Quick Access Toolbar** button to open the **Customize Quick Access Toolbar** menu.

   c) Observe that the **Save**, **Undo**, and **Redo** options are checked, and that these are the buttons that appear in the quick access toolbar.

   d) Check and uncheck the various options to add or remove them from the Quick Access Toolbar.

   e) Select the **Close** button to exit PowerPoint 2010. If prompted to save, select the **Don't Save** button on the **Microsoft PowerPoint** dialog box.

TOPIC B

Create and Save a PowerPoint Presentation

You are now familiar with the various elements of the PowerPoint 2010 user interface, and you are ready to create your first PowerPoint presentation. As you become more familiar with the basic functionality of PowerPoint, you will develop the confidence and the abilities you will need to create high-caliber, high-impact presentations.

To work within PowerPoint 2010, you will need to be able to create a new presentation, add various types of content, and then save and close your file.

The Default PowerPoint Presentation

When you launch PowerPoint 2010, the application opens as a blank presentation with a single slide. This first slide is formatted as a title slide, with text placeholders for a title and a subtitle.

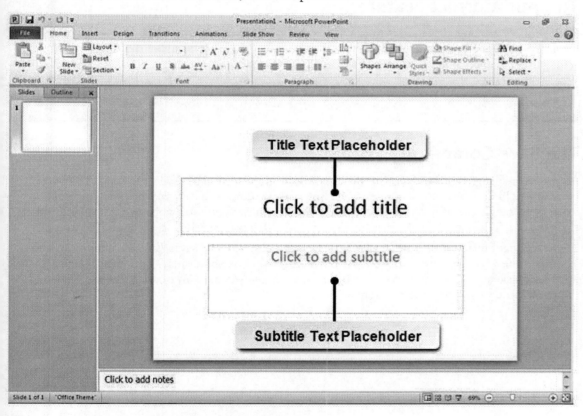

Figure 1-13: The default PowerPoint 2010 presentation.

Text Placeholders

Text placeholders, such as the title and subtitle placeholders in the default first slide, are containers for text. Text placeholders contain instructional text that indicates the type of content that you should enter in them. Text placeholders can be added or removed, resized, moved around the slide, and formatted in various ways. Slides can contain multiple text placeholders.

Notes

As you develop your presentation, you may want to add notes that you can reference when you deliver the presentation before an audience. The *notes pane* allows you to add these speaker notes for each slide in your presentation.

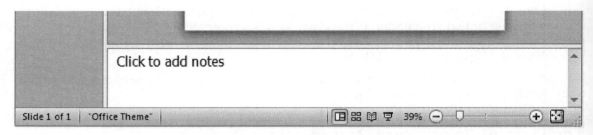

Figure 1-14: The Notes pane.

The AutoCorrect Feature

PowerPoint 2010 includes an *AutoCorrect feature* that corrects common spelling and capitalization errors as you type. This feature can be turned off and on, and you can adjust the AutoCorrect settings. The default state of the AutoCorrect feature is on.

 Note: The AutoCorrect feature will be covered in further detail in Lesson 8.

The Save Command

As you make progress developing your presentation, you will need to save your work. The Save command allows you to save your newly created presentation or to save the changes you make to existing presentations. Once you save a presentation, you can continue working on it or you can close the file. The default file format for PowerPoint 2010 presentations is the .pptx file format.

There are slight differences between saving a new presentation and saving an existing presentation. The first time you save a presentation, the **Save As** dialog box will display. You must select a folder in which to save your file, and give your file a name. When you save an existing file, the file saves to the same location, overwriting the original file.

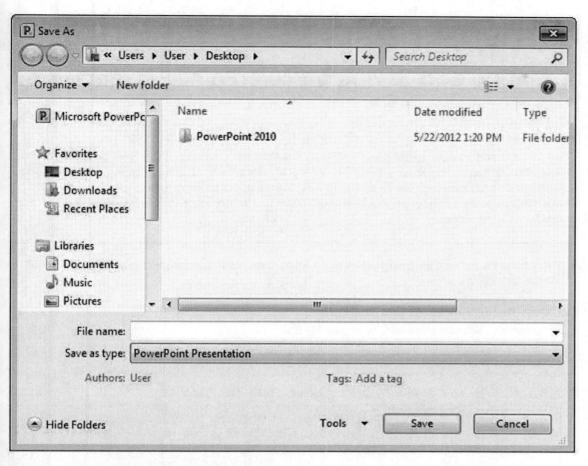

Figure 1-15: The Save As dialog box.

The Save As Command

The Save As command allows you to save a copy of an existing file to an alternate location, save a file with a different file name, or save a file in a different format.

 Access the Checklist tile on your LogicalCHOICE course screen for reference information and job aids on How to Create and Save a PowerPoint Presentation

ACTIVITY 1-2
Creating and Saving a PowerPoint Presentation

Scenario

You have met some of the people on your new team, but not everyone. Your boss feels it would be a good idea for you to introduce yourself at the weekly departmental status meeting. She asks you to put together a brief personal bio so that your new team can get to know you. You decide to use PowerPoint to outline your experiences and qualifications to present to the team. You start by creating a new presentation.

1. Launch the PowerPoint 2010 application by selecting **Start→All Programs→Microsoft Office→Microsoft PowerPoint 2010**.

2. Enter a title and a subtitle for your presentation.
   a) Select the **Title** text placeholder and type **My Bio**.
   b) Select the **Subtitle** text placeholder and type **An Introduction**.
   c) Click anywhere outside the text placeholder to deselect it.

3. Add a slide to your presentation by selecting **Home→Slides→New Slide**.

    Note: This course uses a streamlined notation for ribbon commands. They'll appear as "[Ribbon Tab]→[Group]→[Button or Control]" as in "select **Home→Clipboard→Paste**." If the group name isn't needed for navigation or there isn't a group, it's omitted, as in "select **File→Open**."

4. Add notes to the new slide.
   a) Select the **Notes** pane.
   b) Type a note in the notes pane to remind yourself to discuss projects you have managed.

5. Save your presentation to the desktop.
   a) Select the **File** tab.
   b) Select **Save** or **Save As**.
   c) Select the desktop as the destination for the file.
   d) In the **File name** field, if necessary, type *My Bio*
   e) Select **Save**.
   f) Select **File→Close**.
   g) Verify that there is an icon titled **My Bio.pptx** on the desktop.

TOPIC C

Use Help

As you become more proficient with PowerPoint, and you begin to use more of its advanced features, it is likely that you will come across a command, a menu, or a function with which you are unfamiliar. When that happens, you may be tempted to experiment with the item until you discover how to use it properly, which can result in delays and wasted effort.

PowerPoint contains a built-in help system to assist you in such circumstances. Understanding how PowerPoint's help features work is one of the fastest ways to find answers to your questions. It can also help you become a more proficient PowerPoint user.

PowerPoint Help

PowerPoint Help is a collection of information designed to answer your questions about the various functions of PowerPoint 2010. PowerPoint Help contains articles and multimedia presentations arranged by topic, as well as links to Office.com and a search-for feature for finding additional information within PowerPoint Help, on Office.com, and on other websites.

PowerPoint's main **Help** pane is populated with links to resources that answer some of the most commonly asked questions regarding PowerPoint 2010. You can access PowerPoint Help by clicking the question mark icon to the far right of the ribbon tabs. Alternately, you can press the **F1** key.

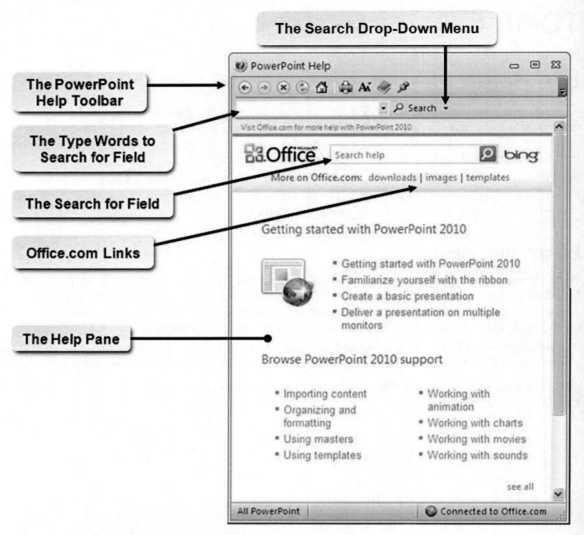

Figure 1-16: The PowerPoint Help dialog box.

The PowerPoint Help Toolbar

The PowerPoint Help toolbar provides you with a quick means of navigating the PowerPoint Help feature.

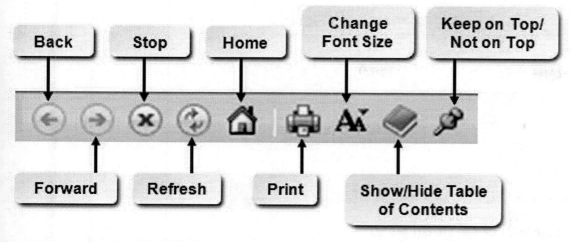

Figure 1-17: The PowerPoint Help toolbar.

PowerPoint Toolbar Button	Function
Back	Navigate to the previous Help page.
Forward	Navigate to the next Help page. This button is only active once the **Back** button has been used.
Stop	Stop an in-progress search.
Refresh	Refresh the displayed page.
Home	Return to the PowerPoint Help home page.
Print	Print the displayed Help page.
Change Font Size	Increase or decrease the size of the font on a Help page.
Show/Hide Table of Contents	Display or hide the **Table of Contents** pane.
Keep on Top/Not on Top	Pins the PowerPoint Help window on top of all other PowerPoint windows, or allows the Help window to be hidden by other PowerPoint windows. This function does not affect other applications.

The Type Words to Search for Field

The **Type words to search for** field and the **Search** drop-down menu work together to tailor your Help search to suit your needs. You can enter terms that you wish to seek help for in the **Type words to search for field**. The **Search** drop-down menu contains various options for narrowing your search.

The Type Words to Search for Field

▼ 🔎 Search ▼

The Search Drop-down Menu

Figure 1-18: Help contains options to narrow your search.

The Search Drop-Down Menu

In addition to selecting between searching for Help topics on your computer and searching for help online, the **Search** drop-down menu provides you with a list of additional options for focusing your search.

Option	Search Result
All PowerPoint	Information on your search query from the PowerPoint Help feature and from the Microsoft Office website. Search results could take you to the Office website.
PowerPoint Help	Same as **All PowerPoint**, but this will not take you out to the Office website.
PowerPoint Templates	Templates that are available from the Office website.
PowerPoint Training	Links to training information on the Office website.
Developer Reference	Resources to help you develop customized PowerPoint presentations.

 Access the Checklist tile on your LogicalCHOICE course screen for reference information and job aids on How to Use PowerPoint Help

ACTIVITY 1–3
Using PowerPoint Help

Scenario
While you were creating your presentation, you noticed some commands and tabs that raised a few questions. You decide to use the **Help** feature to learn more about them.

1. Search for information that would be useful to a new PowerPoint user.

   a) Select the **PowerPoint Help** button ⓐ on the top right of the ribbon.

   b) Select the **Maximize** button ▣ to expand the **PowerPoint Help** window.

   c) Select the **Search** down arrow and, if necessary, select **PowerPoint Help** under **Content from this computer**.

   d) In the **PowerPoint Help** window, select the **Getting Started with PowerPoint** link.

   e) Select the **Familiarize yourself with the ribbon in PowerPoint 2010** link.

   f) Review the information in the **Help** pane.

2. Search for information about the **Backstage View**.

   a) In the **Type words to search for** field, type **Backstage View**.

   b) Select **Search**.

   c) Review the search results.

   d) On the **PowerPoint Help** window, select the **Close** button to exit **Help**.

3. Select **File→Close**.

Summary

In this lesson, you started using Microsoft PowerPoint 2010. You navigated the user interface, created and saved your first PowerPoint presentation, and used the PowerPoint Help feature. Developing these skills provides you with a foundation to build upon. With these skills in hand, you can be confident that you will be able to begin using the more complex features in PowerPoint 2010.

How does your experience using other Microsoft and Microsoft Office applications apply to using PowerPoint 2010? How is PowerPoint 2010 similar to the other applications you have used? How is it different?

Which tasks that you have been assigned in the past would have been easier to accomplish using PowerPoint 2010?

 Note: Check your LogicalCHOICE Course screen for opportunities to interact with your classmates, peers, and the larger LogicalCHOICE online community about the topics covered in this course or other topics you are interested in. From the Course screen you can also access available resources for a more continuous learning experience.

2 | Developing a PowerPoint Presentation

Lesson Time: 1 hour, 20 minutes

Lesson Objectives

In this lesson, you will develop a Microsoft® Office PowerPoint® 2010 presentation. You will:

- Select a presentation type.
- View and navigate a presentation.
- Edit text.
- Build a presentation.

Lesson Introduction

You are now familiar with the basic functions of PowerPoint 2010, and you are ready to develop presentations that you can use in your daily working life. Although you already know how to add slides and basic text to your presentations, you will certainly wish to craft presentations with a bit more substance.

With PowerPoint, you can choose from among several presentation types, apply a variety of themes and templates, and take advantage of powerful text editing capabilities. These allow you to spend less time working on your presentation and more time focusing on your message and how to deliver it.

TOPIC A

Select a Presentation Type

You can now begin developing presentations to deliver key messages to your audience, and you will want to craft those presentations to suit particular situations. PowerPoint offers a wide range of options for customizing and optimizing your presentations, including pre-formatted templates and the ability to create presentations from pre-existing files.

Using these features will allow you to create engaging, dynamic presentations without the time investment required to create presentations from scratch.

Templates

In PowerPoint, a *template* is an existing presentation containing content placeholders that are already formatted. PowerPoint 2010 includes a set of templates that are installed along with the application. You can find additional templates at Office.microsoft.com, or you can create new templates from existing presentations. The file format for PowerPoint templates is the .potx file.

 Note: To further explore templates, you can access the LearnTO **Decide Between PowerPoint Templates and Themes** presentation from the **LearnTO** tile on the LogicalCHOICE Course screen.

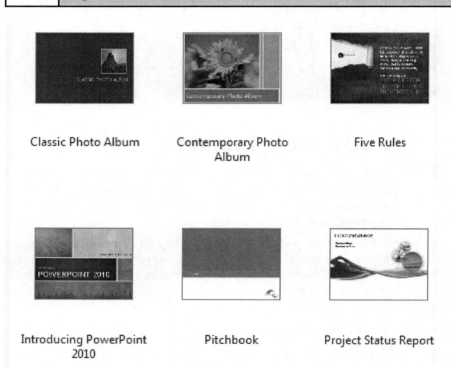

Classic Photo Album   Contemporary Photo Album   Five Rules

Introducing PowerPoint 2010   Pitchbook   Project Status Report

Figure 2-1: PowerPoint 2010 templates.

Project Type Options

There are six options for creating a presentation within PowerPoint.

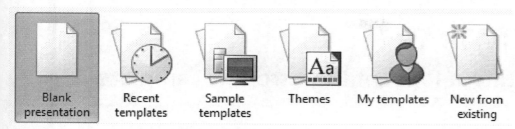

Figure 2-2: Project Type options from the New tab in the Backstage view.

Option	Description
Blank Presentation	Creates a presentation with a single slide that contains only title and subtitle formatting.
Recent Templates	Creates a presentation from a recently used template.
Sample Templates	Creates a presentation from one of the templates included with PowerPoint 2010.
Themes	Creates a presentation from a theme. (Themes will be discussed further in Topic D.)
My Templates	Creates a presentation from a template you have identified as a favorite.
New from Existing	Creates a presentation from an existing presentation.

Outlines

You can also create a PowerPoint presentation from an existing Microsoft Word 2010 outline. The heading styles featured in Word 2010, or any other application that supports heading styles, will create the structure for the presentation. Only the title and the heading text will import to the PowerPoint presentation. Body text from papers and reports authored in Word will not open in the presentation.

 Access the Checklist tile on your LogicalCHOICE course screen for reference information and job aids on How to Select a Presentation Type

ACTIVITY 2–1
Creating a Presentation from a Template

Scenario
You realize that by starting with a blank presentation, you will have to do far more work to put together your brief personal bio. You decide using one of the built-in templates in PowerPoint is a much better starting point for your presentation.

1. Launch PowerPoint 2010.

2. Create your presentation by using a template.
   a) Select File→New to display the **Backstage** view.
   b) In the **Available Templates** pane, select **Sample Templates**.
   c) Select the **Training** template, and then select **Create** in the right pane.

3. Save your presentation to the desktop.
   a) Select File→Save.
   b) Navigate to the desktop in the **Save As** dialog box.
   c) In the **File name** field, type *My Bio*
   d) Select **Save**.
   e) In the **Microsoft PowerPoint** dialog box, select **Yes** to overwrite the existing file.

4. Close the PowerPoint application.

5. Re-open your saved presentation.
   a) Double-click the **My Bio.pptx** icon on the desktop.
   b) Observe that the title bar displays the name "My Bio."
   c) Observe that the status bar displays "Training" as the currently applied template.

TOPIC B

View and Navigate a Presentation

You can now tailor your PowerPoint presentations to suit a variety of needs. As you develop these presentations, you will discover that it is sometimes necessary to reorganize or edit your work. This may not always be easy in the default PowerPoint view, as presentations can contain dozens of slides.

PowerPoint 2010 offers you a variety of options for viewing and navigating your presentations that can make the task of reviewing, reorganizing, and editing your projects far easier. The viewing options allow you to focus on only the types of changes you need to make, by presenting your content in a variety of formats.

Presentation Views

There are four main viewing options in PowerPoint 2010: **Normal**, **Slide Sorter**, **Notes Page**, and **Reading** view. You can access these view options via the buttons in the **Presentation Views** group on the **View** tab.

Presentation View	Description
Normal	Displays all of the slides in a presentation in the **Slides** tab of the left pane. The selected slide appears in the slide pane. This is the default view in PowerPoint.
Slide Sorter	Displays all of the slides in a presentation as large thumbnails. This view is ideal for rearranging slides.
Notes Page	Displays slides and the contents of the speaker notes in page format. This view is ideal for reviewing and editing speaker notes.
Reading	Displays the slides on screen, one at a time. This view is similar to the final presentation your will show to your audience.

Master Views

There are three additional views available in the **View** tab on the ribbon: the **Slide Master** view, the **Handout Master** view, and the **Notes Master** view. The master views are the main slides that store formatting information about the entire presentation. Working with master views allows you to make universal changes to every slide, handout, or notes page associated with a presentation. You can access these views on the **Master Views** group in the **View** tab.

 Note: To further explore slide masters, you can access the LearnTO **Use PowerPoint Slide Masters** presentation from the **LearnTO** tile on the LogicalCHOICE Course screen.

Figure 2–3: Master views.

The Slide Show View

A *slide show* displays your slides on screen in a particular sequence. Slide shows are how you present your slides to the audience. Slide shows display one slide at a time, allowing the audience to follow the key points of a presentation and review textual information, graphics, charts, tables, animations, and videos.

PowerPoint 2010 provides you with a variety of options for presenting your slides via slide shows. You can access these options on the **Slide Show** tab on the ribbon.

Figure 2-4: The Slide Show tab.

Slide Show Options

PowerPoint 2010 gives you a variety of options for viewing and controlling your slide shows.

Viewing Option	Mouse Action	Keyboard Shortcut
Start slide show from the beginning	Click the **From Beginning** button in the Start Slide Show group.	Press **F5**.
Start slide show from the current slide	Click the **From Current Slide** button in the **Start Slide Show** group, or click the **Slide Show** button on the status bar.	Press **Shift+F5**.
Go to a specific slide	While in a slide show, right-click the screen, select **Go to Slide** from the pop-up menu, and then select the desired slide from the secondary pop-up menu.	Press **<the slide number> +Enter**.
Advance to the next slide	Click the screen. Alternately, you can right-click the screen, and then click **Next** in the pop-up menu.	Press any one of the following keys: **N, Enter, Page Down**, the **Right Arrow**, the **Down Arrow**, or the **Spacebar**.
Return to the previous slide	Right-click the screen, and then click **Previous** in the pop-up menu.	Press any one of the following keys: **P, Page Up**, the **Left Arrow**, the **Up Arrow**, or **Backspace**.
Black out the slide show	N/A	Press the **B** key.
White out the slide show	N/A	Press the **W** key.
End a slide show	Right-click the screen, and then choose **End Show** from the pop-up menu.	Press the **Esc** key.

Note: Blacking or whiting out the slide show can be useful when engaging in longer-form conversations. You can draw the audience's attention away from the slides without having to exit the slide show.

The Protected View

In the **Protected View**, the editing options for the presentation are disabled. In PowerPoint 2010, all presentation files from a potentially unsafe source, such as an email attachment or the internet, open in the **Protected View** by default. When the presentation opens, the **Trust** bar will display a warning message that you're viewing the file in the Protected view below the tabs. To enable the editing options and close the Protected view, click the **Enable Editing** button on the **Trust** bar.

Figure 2-5: The Trust bar indicates the presentation is open in the Protected view.

 Access the Checklist tile on your LogicalCHOICE course screen for reference information and job aids on How to View and Navigate a Presentation

ACTIVITY 2–2
Viewing and Navigating a Presentation

Before You Begin

My Bio.pptx is open.

Scenario

You have created your presentation by using the Training template. You understand that much of the existing content and many of the slides will not pertain to your bio. You decide to examine the slides in the presentation to determine which slides you can use.

1. View the first three slides in the **Normal** view.
   a) Select **View→Presentation Views→Normal**. Observe that slide 1 is selected in the left pane, and that slide 1 is also displayed in the slide pane.
   b) Select **slide 2** in the left pane to review it in the slide pane.
   c) Select **slide 3** in the left pane to view it in the slide pane.

2. View the presentation in the **Slide Sorter** view.
   a) Select **View→Presentation Views→Slide Sorter**.
   b) Use the scroll bar or keyboard shortcuts to view the slides.
   c) Scroll up to slide 1, and then double-click **slide 1** to view it in the **Normal** view again.

3. View slide 1 in the **Notes Page** view.
   a) Ensure slide 1 is selected in the left pane.
   b) Observe that there is a large amount of text in the notes pane, and that a scroll bar is displayed to the right.

   c) Select **View→Presentation Views→Notes Page**.
   d) Observe that the slide and all of the text in the notes pane are displayed.

4. View a slide show of the presentation.
   a) Select **Slide Show→Start Slide Show→From Beginning**, or select the **Slide Show** button on the status bar.
   b) Click the screen, or use keyboard shortcuts to advance through the slides.
   c) Right-click the screen. In the pop-up menu, select **Go To Slide**, and then select **14 Case Study** to jump to slide 14.
   d) Press the **B** key to black out the presentation, and then press the **B** key again to restore the presentation.
   e) Press the **Esc** key or right-click the screen and select **End Show** to exit the slide show.
   f) Select **View→Presentation Views→Normal** to return to the **Normal** view.

TOPIC C

Edit Text

Text is one of the most critical elements of any presentation. It is the basic method by which you will deliver the information your audience needs. As you develop your presentation, you are likely to encounter changes that you would like to make. And, let's face it, we all make mistakes. You will need to make some revisions to the text in your presentation.

Knowing how to enter and edit text will enable you to correct errors, focus your message, and deliver your presentation effectively. PowerPoint also gives you the ability to use existing text from other slides and documents to save precious development time.

Text Boxes

It may be necessary to insert additional containers for the text on the slides in your presentation. *Text boxes* are text containers that you add to a slide outside of the default text placeholders for a particular slide layout. Unlike text placeholders, text boxes contain no instructional text; text boxes are blank when you add them to a slide.

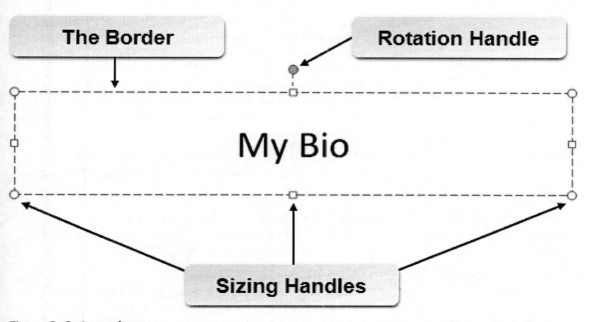

Figure 2-6: A text box.

Like text placeholders, text boxes can be added or removed, resized, moved around the slide, and formatted in various ways. Text placeholders can contain multiple lines of text. By default, typed text will wrap down to the next line when it reaches the text placeholder border. The vertical height of the text placeholder and the text's font size will automatically adjust when the amount of text exceeds the text placeholder's borders. However, you do have the option to lock the font size within a text placeholder.

 Note: Most of the text you will add to your presentations, title text, subtitle text, general body text, bullet lists, and so on, will be added within text boxes. However, other objects, such as shapes, can also contain text.

The Sizing Handles

You can use the *sizing handles* to increase or decrease the size of a text box. By clicking and dragging the sizing handles, you will adjust the size of the text box. The sizing handles on the corners of the text box will adjust both its vertical and horizontal borders simultaneously.

The Rotation Handle

You can use the *rotation handle* to rotate text boxes. Text within the text box will rotate with it.

 Access the Checklist tile on your LogicalCHOICE course screen for reference information and job aids on How to Add and Remove Text Boxes

Text Selection Methods

PowerPoint offers you several options for selecting the text you wish to edit. Selected text will appear highlighted on the screen.

Text Selection	Method
Specific section of text	• Click and drag with the mouse to select a section of text. • Place the insertion point to the left of the text you wish to begin highlighting. Then, press and hold down the **Shift** key and click to the right of the last character of text you wish to highlight. • Place the insertion point next to the text you wish to begin highlighting. Then, press and hold down the **Shift** key and use the arrow keys to extend the highlighted portion of text in any direction.
A single word	Double-click the word. This will also highlight the space following the selected word, but it will not highlight punctuation.
A paragraph or a bulleted item	Triple-click the text.
Noncontiguous sections of text (sections of text that are not adjacent)	Use any of the text selection methods to highlight the first section of text you wish to select. Then, press and hold the **Ctrl** key, and then select the next desired section of text.
All text within a selected text placeholder	• Press **Ctrl+A**. • Click **Home**. Then, in the **Editing** group, click **Select** and click **Select All** from the drop-down menu.

The Mini Toolbar

The *Mini toolbar* is a floating toolbar that appears next to highlighted text. The Mini toolbar allows you to access some of the most commonly used text edit options without having to navigate to them on the ribbon. The Mini toolbar will disappear as you move the mouse pointer away from it or the selected text. You can also access the Mini toolbar by right-clicking anywhere in a text placeholder.

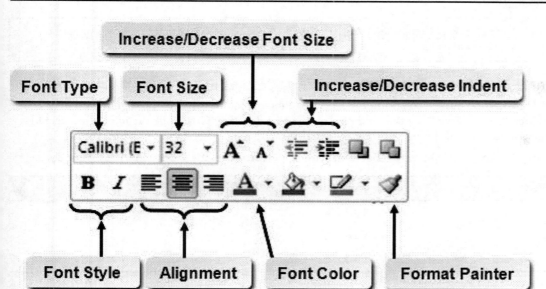

Figure 2-7: The Mini toolbar.

Note: The Mini toolbar will also appear when you right-click certain objects, such as tables. It also appears with different commands for objects such as pictures and charts.

Cut, Copy, and Paste Options

PowerPoint offers you a variety of methods for moving selected text around on slides, from one slide to another, or from other sources into your presentation. To move text within your presentation, you can access the **Cut**, **Copy**, and **Paste** buttons in the **Clipboard** group on the **Home** tab.

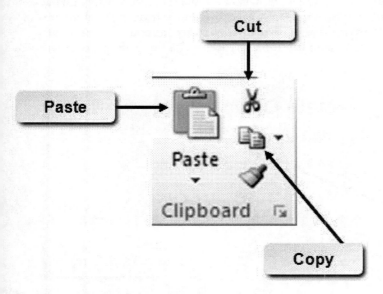

Figure 2-8: The Clipboard group.

The **Cut** button will remove the selected text, whereas the **Copy** button will copy the text but leave the original text in place. Both of these options place a temporary copy of the text on the clipboard. You can then place a copy of the text in a new location in any text placeholder within your presentation.

Note: The Cut, Copy, and Paste functions are the same for slides, and for objects other than text, including text boxes.

Alternate Methods to Cut, Copy, and Paste

Selected text can be moved to another location by dragging and dropping the highlighted text to the desired location, effectively cutting and pasting the text. Holding **Ctrl** while dragging the selected text will place a copy of the text in the new location.

There are also keyboard shortcuts that allow you to perform the Cut, Copy, and Paste functions.

Function	Keyboard Shortcut
Cut	**Ctrl+X**
Copy	**Ctrl+C**
Paste	**Ctrl+V**

The Clipboard

Anything you cut or copy in Office 2010 applications is stored on a task pane called the *clipboard*. You can view the clipboard by clicking the **Clipboard dialog box launcher** in the **Clipboard** group on the **Home** tab. All items on the clipboard, whether from your presentation, other PowerPoint presentations, or other Office applications, are available for pasting into your presentation.

Clicking an item on the clipboard will paste that item to the insert point in your presentation. The **Paste All** button will paste all of the items on the clipboard to the insert point, and the **Clear All** button will delete all items from the clipboard.

Other Clipboard Paste Options

It is likely that not all of the text within your presentation will have the same formatting. Likewise, text copied to the clipboard from other applications may have different formatting than the text in your presentation. The clipboard offers you several paste options to accommodate these textual differences. You can access the clipboard **Paste Options** by clicking the **Paste** drop-down arrow in the **Clipboard** group.

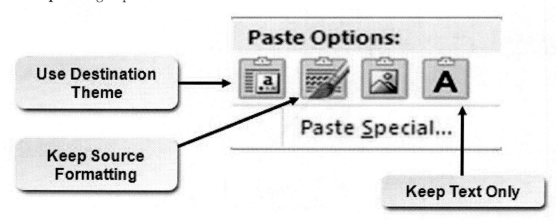

Figure 2-9: The clipboard paste options.

Paste Option	Effect
Use Destination Theme	The pasted text will adopt the formatting of the theme applied to the destination text box.

Paste Option	Effect
Keep Source Formatting	The pasted text retains its original formatting.
Keep Text Only	Only unformatted text is pasted.

The Paste Preview Option

Paste Preview is an option that gives you a temporary preview of a paste command. The paste preview is displayed at the insertion point on a slide when you hover the mouse pointer over a paste option in the **Paste** drop-down list. As you hover over the different options, the preview displays how each would appear if selected.

The Paste Special Command

The *Paste Special command* allows you to paste items to a new location as a specific type of file. For example, you can paste a .jpg file to your presentation as a .png file. You can access the **Paste Special** command on the **Paste Options** drop-down menu in the **Clipboard** group. The **Paste Special** dialog box provides you with the paste options for the selected item.

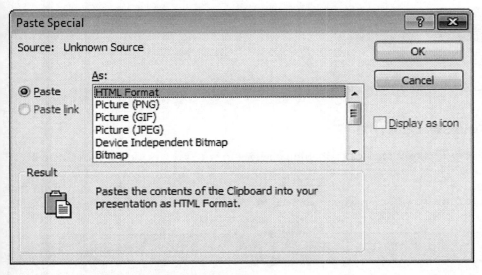

Figure 2-10: The Paste Special dialog box.

Galleries

Galleries are rectangular menus that display a variety of related visual options. These options appear as thumbnail images and provide you with sets of predefined styles for art, pictures, and text that you can apply to your presentation.

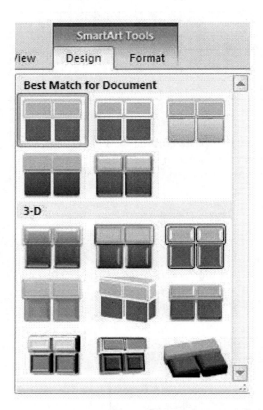

Figure 2-11: A gallery in PowerPoint 2010.

The Live Preview Feature

The *Live Preview feature* displays a view of formatting changes to your presentation without actually applying the changes. These previews appear when you hover the mouse pointer over the various options in some galleries. The preview disappears when you move the mouse pointer away from the option. This feature can save you time when you need to create a highly stylized presentation.

 Access the Checklist tile on your LogicalCHOICE course screen for reference information and job aids on How to Edit Text

ACTIVITY 2-3
Editing Text

Data Files

Dexter_Collingsworth_Resume.docx

Before You Begin

The My Bio.pptx file is open.

The Microsoft Word 2010 application is installed.

Scenario

The Training template is a good starting point for your presentation, but you will need to make changes. You decide to revise some of the text and include information from your résumé.

---

1. Change the title text on the title slide.
   a) Navigate to slide 1 in the left pane.
   b) Select the title text box.
   c) Select the text **Training New Employees**.
   d) Replace the text by typing *My Bio* in the text box.
   e) Click outside the title text box to deselect it.

2. Delete the subtitle text box.
   a) Select the subtitle text to activate the text box.
   b) Select the text box border, which will change the dotted line border into a solid line border.
   c) Press the **Delete** key.

3. Add text to the text box that was behind the subtitle text box.
   a) Select the text box.
   b) Type *An Introduction* into the text box.
   c) Click outside the text box to deselect it.

4. Delete the text in the notes pane.

5. Navigate to slide 2 in the left pane.

6. Replace the text in the title text box with *My Skills*.

7. Copy and paste text from the resume document.
   a) From the Windows desktop, select **Start→All Programs→Microsoft Office→Microsoft Word 2010**.
   b) Select **File→Open**.
   c) In the **Open** dialog box, navigate to the C:\091031Data\Developing a PowerPoint Presentation folder.
   d) Select the Dexter _Collingsworth_Resume.docx file, and then select **Open**.
   e) Select all of the bullet list text in the **Technical Skills** section of the document and then, in the **Clipboard** group, select **Copy**.
   f) Switch back to My Bio.pptx.
   g) Select the text box with the bullet list.
   h) Select all of the bullet list text in the text box.

        i)   Select **Home→Clipboard→Paste down arrow**, and then select **Use Destination Theme** from the drop-down menu.

        j)   Click outside the text box to deselect it.

8. Rearrange the text on the slide.

    a)   Select the text box with the bullet list.

    b)   Select the text in the second bullet point by triple-clicking the text.

    c)   Press and hold the **Ctrl** key.

    d)   While holding the **Ctrl** key, click and drag the text by moving the mouse pointer immediately before the word "Working" in the first bullet point.

    e)   Release the mouse button to place a copy of the selected text at the top of the bullet list, and then release the **Ctrl** key.

    f)   Verify that the same text appears in the first and the third bullets.

    g)   Select the original version of the text (now the third bullet) by triple-clicking the text, and then press the **Delete** key.

    h)   Select the text in the third bullet point by triple-clicking the text.

    i)   Click and drag the text by moving the mouse pointer immediately before the word "Working" in the second bullet point.

    j)   Release the mouse button to switch the position of the second and third bullets.

    k)   Verify that the second and third bullets are now switched.

    l)   Click outside the text box to deselect it.

9. Select **File→Save**.

10. Close Microsoft Word without saving any changes.

TOPIC D

Build a Presentation

As you develop your presentation, it will naturally increase in size and complexity. You will likely need to add additional information, use slides of varying styles, rearrange your slides, and decide on a visual theme for your overall presentation. The more highly developed and fine-tuned you make your presentation, the greater its impact will be on your audience.

With a large amount of the textual content already in place, you will now begin to think more about the big picture. A well organized and professional-looking presentation will only add to your authority and credibility as a presenter.

Slide Layouts

Throughout your presentation, you will likely need to include different types of information on various slides. PowerPoint 2010 includes a selection of *slide layouts* that allow you to organize different types of content in a logical and visually appealing manner. A slide layout is a template that determines the placement of different types of content on an slide.

You can select slide layouts as you add slides to your presentation. You can also apply slide layouts to existing slides. Placeholders for items such as text, tables, charts, and images are built into the various slide layouts.

Types of Slide Layouts

PowerPoint includes nine standard slide layouts that you can add to your presentation.

Slide Layout	What It Includes
Title Slide	Text placeholders for a title and a subtitle.
Title and Content	A text placeholder for a slide title, and a content placeholder for content such as text, images, graphs, charts, or clip art.
Section Header	Text placeholders for section and subsection titles.
Two Content	A text placeholder for a slide title, and two content placeholders for a variety of content types.
Comparison	Text placeholder for a slide title, two text placeholders for subtitles, and two content placeholders for a variety of content types.
Title Only	A text placeholder to enter a slide title.
Blank	No placeholders.
Content with Caption	A text placeholder for a slide title, a text placeholder for textual content, and a content placeholder for a variety of content types.
Picture with Caption	A picture placeholder and a text placeholder for caption text.

Slide Size and Orientation

In addition to selecting from the various layouts, PowerPoint 2010 gives you the ability to modify the size and the orientation of your slides. The default size of the PowerPoint slide is 10 inches by 7.5 inches. This is in the 4:3 aspect ratio, which is the format for standard definition television broadcasts. Other sizes, such as the 16:9 widescreen format and 35mm slides, are also available. You can also switch between the default landscape orientation and portrait orientation.

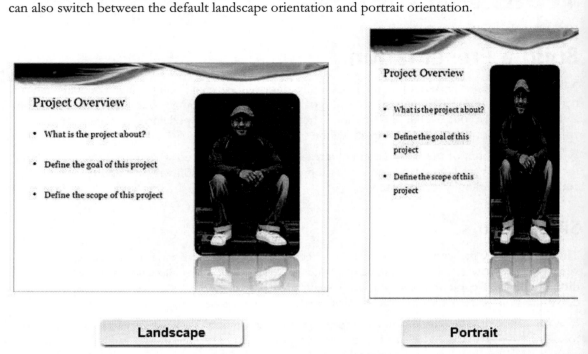

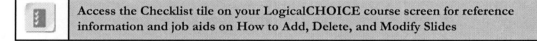

Figure 2-12: PowerPoint slides in the landscape and portrait orientations.

> Access the Checklist tile on your LogicalCHOICE course screen for reference information and job aids on How to Add, Delete, and Modify Slides

ACTIVITY 2-4
Adding, Deleting, and Modifying Slides

Data Files
Project Team.pptx

Before You Begin
My Bio.pptx is open.

Scenario
You decide you would like to add slides with the Section Header layout to introduce various sections of your presentation. You also remember that a colleague from school used a picture of you in a PowerPoint presentation that she put together for an old project. You think the image would be appropriate for your bio, so you decide to use the slide in your current presentation, and to delete the slides you will not need.

1. Add a slide that has the Section Header layout.
   a) Ensure the presentation is in the **Normal** view.
   b) Navigate to slide 1 in the left pane.
   c) Select **Home→Slides→New Slide down arrow** to view the **Slide Layout** gallery.
   d) Select the **Section Header** layout.
   e) Select the title text box, and replace the "Click To Edit Master Title Style" with *My Experience*.
   f) Select the **Company Logo** box below the title text box, and then press the **Delete** key to delete it.

2. Duplicate the slide you just added.
   a) Ensure that slide 2 is selected in the left pane.
   b) Select **Home→Clipboard→Copy down arrow**.
   c) Select **Duplicate** from the drop-down menu.
   d) Select the "**My Experience**" text.
   e) Delete "My Experience," and then type *My Qualifications* in the text box.

3. Reuse the slide with your picture.
   a) Select **Home→Slides→New Slide down arrow**.
   b) From the **New Slide** drop-down menu, select **Reuse Slides**.
   c) From the **Reuse Slides** pane, select the **Browse** button, and then select **Browse file**.
   d) Navigate to C:\091031Data\Developing a PowerPoint Presentation in the **Browse** dialog box.
   e) Select the Project Team.pptx file, and then select **Open**.
   f) In the **Reuse Slides** pane, select slide 2 from the **Slides** pane.
   g) Select the **Close** button to close the **Reuse Slides** pane.

4. Delete a series of slides.
   a) Select slide 6 from the left pane.
   b) Press and hold down the **Shift** key, and then select slide 9.
   c) Press the **Delete** key.
   d) Select and delete slides 7 through 14.

5. Delete noncontiguous slides.
   a) Select slide 8 from the left pane.

b) Press and hold down the **Ctrl** key.

c) Select slide 10, and then press the **Delete** key.

6. Select **File→Save**, and then select **File→Close**.

 Access the Checklist tile on your LogicalCHOICE course screen for reference information and job aids on How to Arrange Slides

ACTIVITY 2–5
Arranging Slides

Data Files
Bio_modified.pptx

Before You Begin
The PowerPoint 2010 application is open.

Scenario
You have finished creating the slides you will need for the presentation during the team meeting. You realize you have included all pertinent information for a brief professional bio, but you have not arranged the slides in the proper order. You will need to organize your slides in a logical manner before presenting to your new team.

---

1. Open the Bio_modified.pptx file from the C:\091031Data\Developing a PowerPoint Presentation folder.

2. Move a slide in the **Normal** view.
   a) Ensure the presentation is in the **Normal** view.
   a) Scroll down and select slide 9 in the left pane.
   b) From the **Clipboard** group, select **Cut**.
   c) Scroll up and select slide 2.
   d) From the **Clipboard** group, select the **Paste** button to insert the slide after slide 2.
   e) Observe that slide 9 is now slide 3, and that all of the subsequent slides have been moved down one place in the slide order.

3. Arrange the remaining slides in the **Slide Sorter** view.
   a) Select **View→Presentation Views→Slide Sorter**.
   b) Select slide 6, and then drag and drop it after slide 3.
   c) Verify that slide 6 is now slide 4.
   d) Select both slide 6 and slide 7.
   e) Drag and drop slides 6 and 7 to appear after slide 8.

4. Review the order of your slides.
   a) In the **Presentation Views** group, select the **Normal** button.
   b) Navigate through the slides to ensure they are in a logical order.

5. Save the file in the current folder as *My Bio_modified.pptx*

Themes

Themes are combinations of colors, fonts, and effects that give your presentation a consistent look and feel throughout. Themes help to define the background color of slides and the color and style of objects such as charts and tables. You can apply themes to individual slides, groups of slides, or your entire presentation.

Note: To further explore themes, you can access the LearnTO **Decide Between PowerPoint Templates and Themes** presentation from the **LearnTO** tile on the LogicalCHOICE Course screen.

 Note: Developing and customizing themes is a multi-faceted endeavor that can benefit from large-scale collaboration. If your instructor/organization is incorporating social media resources as part of this training, use the LogicalCHOICE Course screen to search for or begin conversations regarding successes and challenges encountered while designing themes for your presentations.

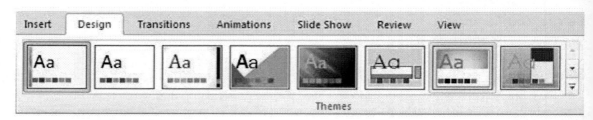

Figure 2–13: PowerPoint themes.

Quick Styles

Quick styles are themes that can quickly be applied to a particular object on a slide by selecting a single command button. Quick styles are found in galleries and often appear in contextual tabs when objects such as charts or graphs are selected.

Theme Components

The three visual components of themes are colors, fonts, and effects. While themes contain pre-determined attributed for these components, you can customize them to suit your needs.

Theme Component	Description
Color	Theme colors determine the color applied to particular on-slide elements. You can customize theme colors on the **Colors** drop-down menu in the **Themes** group.
Font	Themes apply a different font to title text and the body text on slides. You can select different fonts on the **Fonts** drop-down menu in the **Themes** group.
Effects	Themes apply effects, such as drop shadows and beveled edges, to on-slide elements. You can change these effects on the **Effects** drop-down menu in the **Themes** group.

Background Styles

Background styles are the colors and textures of slide backgrounds. These are determined by applying themes to your slides. You can select additional backgrounds from the gallery on the **Background Styles** drop-down menu on the **Background** group.

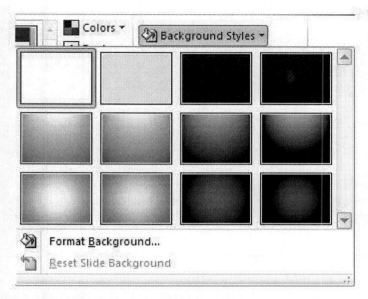

Figure 2-14: The Background styles gallery.

Hide Background Graphics

You can hide any graphics that appear in the background of a slide by clicking the **Hide Background Graphics** check box in the **Background** group.

If you apply a theme to a presentation and the style does not appear to change on certain slides, you might need to hide background images to view the actual slide backgrounds.

 Note: This feature does not apply to background fills.

The Format Background Dialog Box

You can find options for customizing the backgrounds of slides, beyond the available Quick styles, in the **Format Background** dialog box. You can access the **Format Background** dialog box from the **Background Styles** gallery, or from the dialog box launcher on the Background group. The options for formatting backgrounds appear on four tabs.

Tab Option	Allows You To
Fill	Access options for creating solid, gradient, picture or texture, and pattern fills. You can also adjust various attributes for fills, such as brightness, transparency, and color.
Picture Corrections	Adjust the attributes, such as sharpness, brightness, and contrast, of pictures that are being used as backgrounds. The Reset button restores the default settings for brightness and contrast.
Picture Color	Adjust the color saturation and the color tone of your background.
Artistic Effects	Customize your slide backgrounds with various artistic effects.

Access the Checklist tile on your LogicalCHOICE course screen for reference information and job aids on How to Work with Themes

ACTIVITY 2-6
Working with Themes

Before You Begin

The My Bio_modified.pptx file is open.

Scenario

Your bio is nearly complete, but you don't like the overall look of the presentation and you would like to give it some pizzazz. You decide to spruce up the original template by changing the theme and the background style.

1. Apply a theme to the presentation.
   a) Access the **Design** tab.
   b) Expand the **All Themes** gallery by selecting the **More** button in the **Themes** group.
   c) From the **All Themes** gallery, select the **Slipstream** theme.

   > Note: The themes in the **All Themes** gallery are arranged in alphabetical order.

   d) Observe that the style has been applied to all of the slides; however, slides 1, 4, 7, and 11 contain background images that have not been affected by applying the new theme.

2. Hide the background images for slides 1, 4, 7, and 11.
   a) Ensure the **Design** tab is selected.
   b) Select slides 1, 4, 7, and 11 in the left pane.
   c) In the **Background** group, check the **Hide Background Graphics** check box.
   d) Verify that the background images no longer display.

3. Apply a background style to all slides.
   a) Select slide 1 in the left pane.
   b) In the **Background** group, select **Background Styles** to display the **Background Styles** gallery.
   c) Hover the mouse pointer over the various styles to view the previews. Then, select the desired background style.
   d) Observe that the background style for the entire presentation has been modified.

4. Apply a gradient fill to all slides.
   a) Ensure the **Design** tab is selected.
   b) In the **Background** group, select the **dialog box launcher** to display the **Format Background** dialog box.
   c) If necessary, select the **Gradient fill** radio button to select the gradient fill options.
   d) Select **Preset colors** to display the color scheme menu.
   e) Select the **Horizon** color scheme in the top-right corner of the menu.
   f) Modify the various options to achieve the desired gradient fill.
   g) In the **Format Background** dialog box, select **Apply to All** to apply the gradient fill to all slides.
   h) Select the **Close** button.
   i) Verify that the gradient fill has been applied to all slides.

5. Save and close the file.

Summary

In this lesson, you began developing a PowerPoint presentation. You selected a presentation type, viewed and navigated a presentation, edited text, and built a presentation. Now that you have a solid understanding of the main functions of PowerPoint 2010, you are ready to begin exploring its more advanced features.

How can customizing presentations help you convey your thoughts and ideas more effectively?

As you have worked with PowerPoint 2010, have you discovered alternate methods for performing some of the functions covered in this training? Is this similar to your experience with other Microsoft Office applications?

 Note: Check your LogicalCHOICE Course screen for opportunities to interact with your classmates, peers, and the larger LogicalCHOICE online community about the topics covered in this course or other topics you are interested in. From the Course screen you can also access available resources for a more continuous learning experience.

3 | Performing Advanced Text Editing

Lesson Time: 50 minutes

Lesson Objectives

In this lesson, you will perform advanced text editing. You will:

- Format characters.

- Format paragraphs.

- Format text boxes.

Lesson Introduction

You have begun developing Microsoft® Office PowerPoint® presentations with strong visual appeal and a consistent look and feel. You have mastered the basic building blocks of presentations, and you know how to customize your presentations to suit your particular needs. Now, you will focus on honing your message by utilizing some of the advanced text editing features in PowerPoint 2010.

Not all content carries the same weight. You will need ways to emphasize certain key points, while still presenting all relevant information to your audience. Additionally, you may want to format the text in your presentations to make it easier to read or to have more visual appeal. But, none of this should consume large amounts of your development time. By becoming familiar with some of the advanced text editing features in PowerPoint 2010, you will be able to focus on your message instead of wasting hours of time customizing the appearance of your text.

TOPIC A

Format Characters

Text is likely to be one of your main means of conveying information. As such, it is important to select the best character formatting for your presentations. The proper character formatting will give your presentation a professional appearance while ensuring the audience does not miss out on key information.

Without formatting, the text in your presentations will appear flat. There will be no visual cues for the audience to interpret the text, and the presentation will be just plain boring. You have entered text into your presentations, now you will energize that text.

Character Formats

Character formats are particular attributes that you can apply to the text on your slides. By changing these attributes, you will alter the appearance of the text in your presentation. There are four basic elements of character formats: font type, size, color, and style.

The Font Dialog Box

The Font dialog box provides advanced character formatting options to customize the text in your presentations. You can access the **Font** dialog box by selecting the **dialog box launcher** in the **Font** group on the **Home** tab.

Font Dialog Box Option	Description
Latin Text Font	Allows you to select from any of the included font types in PowerPoint 2010.
Font Style	Allows you to select a font style, such as bold, italic, or regular.
Size	Allows you to modify the size of text on your slides.
Font Color	This drop-down menu opens a gallery of text color options. You can also customize the color of the text in your presentations by clicking **More Colors**.
Underline Style	Allows you to select a style of underline for emphasizing text.
Underline Color	Allows you to select a color for your underlines. You can also customize underline colors.
Effects	Provides a selection of additional textual effects including strikethrough, all caps, and equalize character height.
Character Spacing Tab	Provides options for adjusting the spacing between textual characters.

 Note: Many of the commands in the **Font** dialog box can be accessed via buttons in the **Font** group on the **Home** tab.

WordArt Styles

WordArt styles are predetermined formatting configurations that can be applied to text on a slide. These formatting configurations can be applied to selected text or to all text within a text placeholder. You can access WordArt styles from the **Text** group on the **Insert** tab or from the **WordArt Styles** group on the **Drawing Tools** contextual tab.

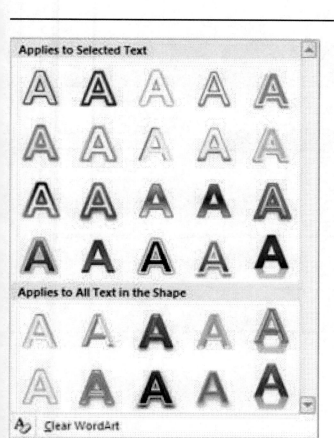

Figure 3-1: The WordArt styles gallery.

The Format Painter

The *Format Painter* allows you to copy the formatting of selected text and apply it to other text. The **Format Painter** functions much like the copy and paste commands, however, only the formatting, and not the text, is moved. You can access the **Format Painter** in the **Clipboard** group on the **Home** tab.

The Replace Fonts Option

The *Replace Fonts* option allows you to easily change all text of a particular font type to another font type throughout an entire presentation. This option can come in handy when you create your presentation on one computer, and then deliver your presentation from another. If the fonts you created your project with don't exist on the computer your deliver your presentation from, this feature can be a lifesaver. You can access the **Replace Fonts** option from the **Replace** drop-down menu in the **Editing** group on the **Home** tab.

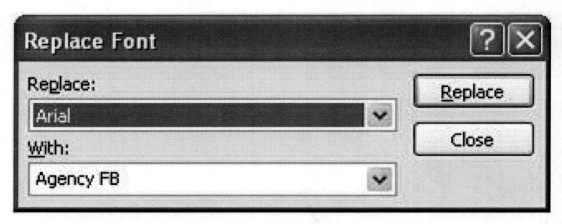

Figure 3-2: The Replace Font dialog box.

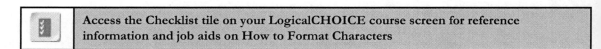

Access the Checklist tile on your LogicalCHOICE course screen for reference information and job aids on **How to Format Characters**

ACTIVITY 3-1
Formatting Characters

Data Files
Bio_theme.pptx

Scenario
The thematic elements you applied to your presentation have made some of the text difficult to read. You decide to change the text formatting to make your presentation easier to read.

1. Open the Bio_theme.pptx file from the C:\091031Data\Performing Advanced Text Editing folder.

2. Change the text font.
   a) Select slide 5 from the left pane.
   b) Select all of the text in the first bullet point.
   c) In the **Font** group, from the **Font** field, select the **down arrow**.
   d) Observe that the current font is **Trebuchet MS**. Select **Arial Black** from the drop-down menu, and then click outside the text box to deselect it.
   e) In the **Editing** group, select the **down arrow** next to the **Replace** button and then select **Replace Fonts**.
   f) In the **Replace Fonts** dialog box, select the **down arrow** on the **Replace** field, and then select **Trebuchet MS** from the drop-down menu.
   g) Select the **down arrow** on the **With** field, and then select **Arial Black** from the drop-down menu.
   h) Select **Replace** and then select **Close**.
   i) Verify that all of the Trebuchet MS text has been replaced with Arial Black for the presentation.

3. Change the color of the text.
   a) Navigate to slide 5.
   b) Select all of the text in the first bullet point, and then hover the mouse pointer over the **Mini toolbar**.
   c) Select the down arrow on the **Font Color** button, and then select **Black, Background 1**, which is the first color in the **Theme Colors** menu.
   d) Select some of the text in the first bullet point, and then select **Format Painter** ✇ Format Painter from the **Clipboard** group.
   e) Select all of the text in the second bullet point to apply the formatting.
   f) Verify that the text in the second bullet point is black.
   g) Apply the same formatting to the third bullet point.

4. Apply WordArt to the title text.
   a) Navigate to slide 1.
   b) Select the "My Bio" title text, and then access the **Drawing Tools** contextual tab.
   c) In the **WordArt Styles** group, select the **More** button ⊟ to display the **WordArt** gallery.
   d) Hover the mouse pointer over the various styles to view the previews, and then select the desired style.

5. Save the file as *My Bio_theme.pptx*, and then close the file.

TOPIC B

Format Paragraphs

Formatting and applying style to your text can make your presentation easier to read and can help you convey your message. But, there is another important aspect of organizing and formatting your textual content: formatting paragraphs. Now that you have tailored your text to have just the right look, you will organize the physical layout of your text by formatting your paragraphs.

The paragraph formatting options in Microsoft® Office PowerPoint® give you the ability to control the overall layout of the text in your presentations. Think of paragraph formatting as how you organize the structure of your textual content.

Bulleted Lists

Bulleted lists are used to display a sequence of items for which the order is not important. Each of the items displays as a line of text with an image, or a bullet, to the left. PowerPoint 2010 allows you to add bulleted lists to your textual content and provides a number of options for formatting them. You can select the appearance of the bullets in your lists, create custom bullets, create bulleted lists with multiple sub-levels, and alter the distance between the margin of the text placeholder and the bullet items in your lists.

To begin a bulleted list, go to the **Home** tab, navigate to the **Paragraph** group, and select the **Bullets** button. You can access the bulleted list formatting options in the **Bullets and Numbering** dialog box, on the **Bulleted** tab.

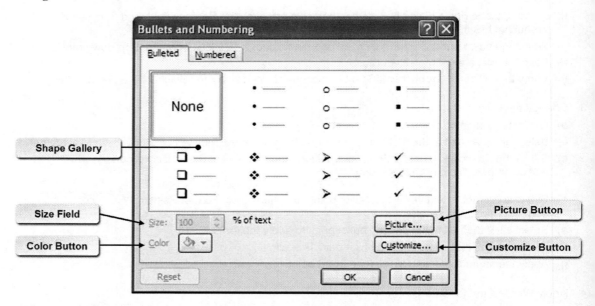

Figure 3–3: The Bullets and Numbering dialog box with the Bulleted tab selected.

Numbered Lists

Use numbered lists to display a series of items for which the order is important, for example, the steps in a process or procedure. As with bulleted lists, PowerPoint 2010 provides you with a number of options for formatting your numbered lists. You can use Arabic or Roman numerals in your numbered lists, as well as letters. This can be useful for presenting high-level outlines to your audience.

To begin a numbered list, go to the **Home** tab, navigate to the **Paragraph** group, and click the **Numbering** button. You can access the numbered list formatting options in the **Bullets and Numbering** dialog box, on the **Numbered** tab.

 Note: You can also apply bulleting or numbering to existing paragraph text. All text separated by a line break will become an individual bullet or numbered item.

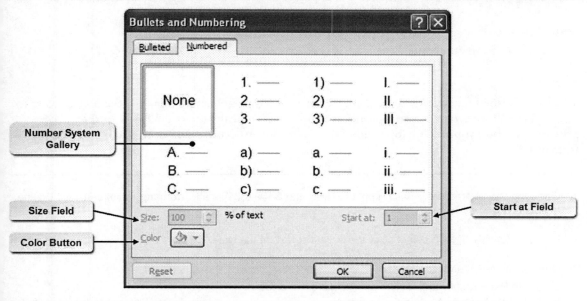

Figure 3–4: The Bullets and Numbering dialog box with the Numbered tab selected.

Option	Allows You To
Number System Gallery	Select from among Arabic numerals, Roman numerals, and letters for your numbered lists.
Size	Set the font size of the numbers or letters as a percentage of the size of the text.
Color	Change the color of the numbers or letters in your numbered list. This does not change the color of the list text.
Start At	Specify the initial number or letter value to begin your numbered lists.

 Access the Checklist tile on your LogicalCHOICE course screen for reference information and job aids on How to Use Bulleted and Numbered Lists

ACTIVITY 3–2
Using Bulleted and Numbered Lists

Data Files

Bio_character formatting.pptx

Scenario

You have finished formatting the text characters for your presentation. You feel the text is easier to read and the WordArt style you applied to the title text better fits the overall look of the presentation. But, you aren't happy with the way the bullets look, so you decide to change the formatting.

1. Open the Bio_character formatting.pptx file from the C:\091031Data\Performing Advanced Text Editing folder.

2. Navigate to slide 5, then select all of the bullet list text on the slide.

3. Change the bullet style for the list.
   a) In the **Paragraph** group, select the **Bullets down arrow**.
   b) Select **Bullets and Numbering** from the drop-down menu to display the **Bullets and Numbering** dialog box.
   c) Select **Star Bullets** as the bullet style.
   d) Select **OK**.

4. Modify the bullet size.
   a) Display the **Bullets and Numbering** dialog box.
   b) Use the **spin buttons** in the **Size** field to change the bullet size to 150% of text.

    Note: Notice that the bullets now outsize their text. Most of the time, you'll want to avoid this in your presentation. This step is meant to make it easier for you to see the change in formatting.

   c) Select **OK**.

5. Change bullets to a numbered list.
   a) Navigate to slide 9.
   b) Select all of the bulleted list text on the slide.
   c) From the **Paragraph** group, select the **Numbering** button.

6. Save the file as *My Bio_character formatting.pptx*, and then close the file.

Text Alignment

PowerPoint offers you several options for aligning the text within text placeholders and other objects. The text alignment options allow you to position the text relative to the margins within the text box or object.

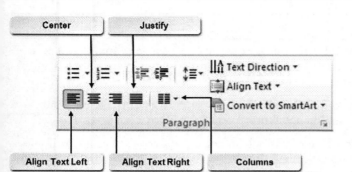

Figure 3-5: Text alignment options.

Option	Result
Align Text Left	Text lines up along the left margin.
Center	Text is centered evenly between the left and right margins.
Align Text Right	Text lines up along the right margin.
Justify	Similar to center alignment, text is centered evenly between the left and the right margins. Additionally, extra spaces between words or characters may be added to square off the text block, providing a uniform look along the left and right edges.
Columns	Creates individual columns for text. Up to 16 columns are available in a text box.

 Note: As with bulleted and numbered lists, you can adjust the margins of standard body text by using the **Decrease List Level** or **Increase List Level** buttons.

Vertical Text Alignment

PowerPoint 2010 also gives you three options for vertically aligning your text. You can access these options by going to the **Home** tab, the **Paragraph** group, and then the **Align Text** drop-down menu.

Option	Text Is
Top	Vertically aligned along the top of the text box
Middle	Centered vertically
Bottom	Vertically aligned along the bottom of the text box

The AutoFit Feature

The *AutoFit feature* gives you options for automatically fitting text within text boxes and other objects regardless of how much text you enter. You can access the AutoFit options in the **Format Text Effects** dialog box, which you can launch from either the **Align Text** [Align Text] or the **Text Direction** [Text Direction] drop-down menu. The default AutoFit setting is **Resize shape to fit the text**.

Option	Effect
Do Not AutoFit	PowerPoint will adjust neither the text nor the text box. If you enter more text than will fit in a text box, the extra text will spill over and appear outside the text box.
Shrink Text on Overflow	PowerPoint will automatically decrease the size of the text if you enter more text than will fit.
Resize Shape to Fit Text	PowerPoint will automatically increase the size of the text box if you enter more text than will fit.

Note: When **Do Not AutoFit** is selected, any text that spills over off of the text box is still associated with the text box. While the text appears outside the border, changes made to the text box will affect the overflow text. For example, if you move the text box, the text will move with it. If you delete the text box, you will also delete the overflow text.

Wrap Text in Shape

When the **Wrap text in shape** check box ☑ Wrap text in shape in the **Format Text Effects** dialog box is checked, text entered into shapes will align to the edges of the shape.

Spacing Options

Spacing refers to the vertical distance between lines of text or paragraphs. There are three spacing attributes that can be adjusted in PowerPoint 2010: line spacing, before, and after. You can quickly adjust the spacing between lines of text via the **Line Spacing** button ⬍≣▾ in the Paragraph group. You can also launch the **Paragraph** dialog box from there.

Spacing Option	Enables You To Adjust
Line Spacing	The spacing between lines of text
Before	Text spacing by adding space before a paragraph
After	Text spacing by adding space after a paragraph

Text Direction Options

In addition to being able to format, align, and space your text, PowerPoint 2010 also gives you the ability to change the direction in which your text flows. The default text direction option is horizontal, but you can also rotate your text or stack it vertically.

Clear All Formatting

You can reset any formatting you perform on text by selecting the text, and then selecting the **Clear All Formatting** button 📑 in the **Font** group on the **Home** tab.

Rulers

Rulers are visual reference tools that allow you to accurately position objects on a slide. The rulers display marked increments that make it easy for you to place objects with precision. You can also use the rulers to adjust margins and indentations of text within objects.

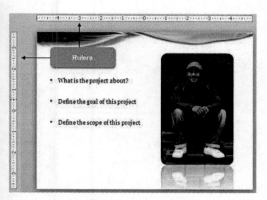

Figure 3-6: Rulers in the slide pane.

 Access the **Checklist** tile on your **LogicalCHOICE** course screen for reference information and job aids on **How to Format Paragraphs**

ACTIVITY 3–3
Formatting Paragraphs

Data Files

Bio_bullet formatting.pptx

Scenario

You have finished reformatting all of the bulleted and numbered lists in your presentation. But, you are not happy with some of the text spacing on your slides. You decide to format some of the paragraphs in your presentation to give it a more well-balanced look.

---

1. Open the Bio_bullet formatting.pptx file from the C:\091031Data\Performing Advanced Text Editing folder.

2. Navigate to slide 2. Modify the horizontal text alignment.
   a) Select the "Dexter Collingsworth" text in the text box.
   b) In the **Paragraph** group, select the **Align Text Right** button.

3. Modify the line spacing.
   a) In the **Paragraph** group, select the **Line Spacing** button.
   b) Select **1.5** from the drop-down menu.
   c) Click outside the text box to deselect it.

4. Navigate to slide 6. Modify the vertical text alignment.
   a) Select all of the text in the bulleted list.
   b) In the **Paragraph** group, select the **Align Text** button and then select **Middle** from the drop-down menu.

5. Modify the indentation of the text.
   a) If the rulers are not visible, select **View→Show→Ruler check box**.
   b) Drag the **Hanging Indent** marker to the right until it is pointing at the 1/2 inch mark on the top ruler.
   c) Click outside the text box to deselect it.

6. Save the file as *My Bio_bullet formatting.pptx*, and then close the file.

TOPIC C

Format Text Boxes

You have selected the perfect text and have it arranged on your slides just the way you like it. But, something still seems a but dull about the way your text looks on screen, and you'd like to spruce it up a bit more. PowerPoint 2010 gives you the option of formatting the text boxes in your presentation by adding color, modifying the borders, or applying a number of effects.

Adding a little style to the text boxes in your presentation can give your textual content that added boost to keep the audience engaged. Text box formatting gives you the ability to add variety to your text and set it off from other on-slide elements. This draws the audience's attention where you want it, on your key points.

Text Formatting Options

There are three general categories of text placeholder formatting options: fill, outline, and effects. You will find these options on the **Home** tab in the **Drawing** group. Formatting options for text boxes, text placeholders, and shapes are the same.

 Note: You can use the **Format Painter** to copy and paste text box formatting as well as text formatting.

Figure 3–7: Text formatting options.

 Note: Inserting and working with shapes will be covered in Lesson 4.

Shape Fills

As with slide backgrounds, you can add fills to the text boxes in your presentations. The **Shape Fill** drop-down menu provides you with options for adding color, pictures, gradient fills, and textures as backgrounds for your text boxes.

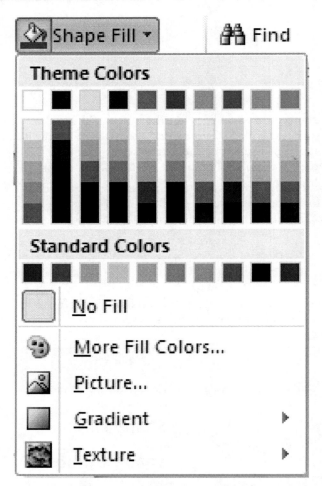

Figure 3-8: The Shape Fill drop-down menu.

Shape Outlines

Text boxes are objects that are contained within a slide. As such, they have borders, or outlines, to separate them from other content on the slide. PowerPoint gives you an array of options for formatting the outlines of text boxes and other shapes. You can access these options in the **Shape Outline** drop-down menu.

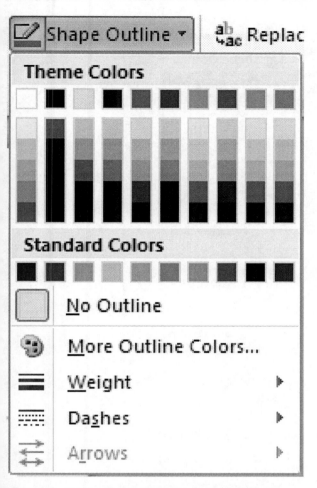

Figure 3-9: The Shape Outline drop-down menu.

Option	Allows You To
Color	Select the color of the outline
Weight	Set the line width of the outline
Dashes	Select from among various styles of dashed lines for the outline

Shape Effects

PowerPoint 2010 allows you to select from a variety of effects for text boxes and shapes, such as beveled or soft edges, 3-D rotation, and the addition of drop shadows. Each type of effect has an associated gallery with pre-formatted options. You can also customize the effects to suit your needs. You can access the effects options from the **Shape Effects** drop-down menu.

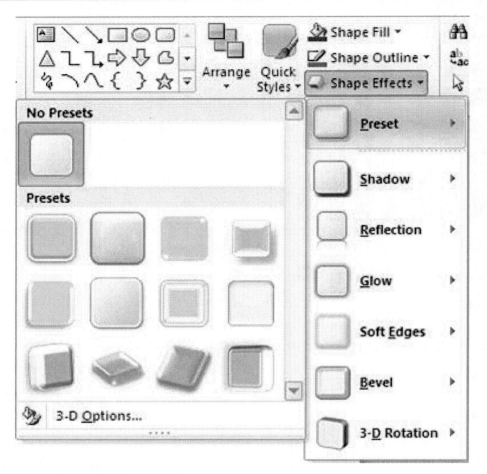

Figure 3–10: The Shape Effects drop-down menu.

 Access the Checklist tile on your LogicalCHOICE course screen for reference information and job aids on How to Format Text Boxes

ACTIVITY 3–4
Formatting Text Boxes

Data Files

Bio_paragraph formatting.pptx

Scenario

You have finished formatting the paragraphs in your presentation. Although you are happy with the overall look of the text, you feel the text boxes could look better. You decide to format the text boxes to give your presentation a more well-polished look.

1. Open the Bio_paragraph formatting.pptx file from the C:\091031Data\Performing Advanced Text Editing folder.

2. Navigate to slide 5. Add a fill to the text box.
   a) Select the text box.
   b) Select the **Shape Fill** button in the **Drawing** group.
   c) Select a light blue color from the **Theme Colors** section of the drop-down menu.
   d) Select the **Shape Fill** button from the **Drawing** group, and then select **Gradient** from the drop-down menu.
   e) Select a gradient variation from the gallery.
   f) Select the **Drawing** group's **dialog box launcher** to display the **Format Shape** dialog box.
   g) In the **Gradient stops** section, drag the lever to modify the look of the gradient fill.

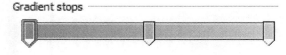
Gradient stops

 Note: Each **Gradient stop** affects one color of the gradient fill. The options below the **Gradient stops** affect only the color of the selected gradient stop. You must select the formatting options for each color in a gradient fill separately.

   h) Use the **Transparency spin button** to set the transparency to 25%.
   i) Select **Close** to view the results of your formatting.

3. Format the outline of the text box.
   a) Select the **Drawing** group's **dialog box launcher** to display the **Format Shape** dialog box.
   b) Select the **Line Color** tab, and then select the **Solid line** radio button.
   c) Select the **Color** button, and then select a dark red color from the **Theme Colors** section of the drop-down menu.

 Note: The border that appears because the text box is selected might mask some of the text box border formatting as you work.

   d) Select the **Line Style** tab.
   e) In the **Line Style** section, use the **spin buttons** to set the **Width** to 3pt.
   f) Select the **Close** button.

4. Apply an effect to the text box.

    a) Select the **Shape Effects** button from the **Drawing** group, and then select **Shadow**.

    b) From the **Perspective** section in the **Shadow** gallery, select **Perspective Diagonal Upper Left**. This is the first tile in the **Perspective** section.

5. Save the file as *My Bio_paragraph formatting.pptx*, and close the file.

Summary

In this lesson, you formatted text characters, paragraphs, and text boxes. Your text is now well organized and easy to read. Perhaps most importantly, your text will grab the audience's attention and focus it on the key points of your message. Now, you are ready to add multimedia components to your presentation, bringing it up to the next level.

How can you use the text editing and formatting features in PowerPoint 2010 to help convey your message?

Which of the text editing and formatting features do you find most useful?

 Note: Check your LogicalCHOICE Course screen for opportunities to interact with your classmates, peers, and the larger LogicalCHOICE online community about the topics covered in this course or other topics you are interested in. From the Course screen you can also access available resources for a more continuous learning experience.

4 | Adding Graphical Elements to Your Presentation

Lesson Time: 30 minutes

Lesson Objectives

In this lesson, you will add graphical elements to your presentation. You will:

- Insert clip art and images.

- Insert shapes.

Lesson Introduction

You are now able to create and organize your presentation. You can also use the powerful PowerPoint 2010 text editing features to drive your point home. But text isn't the only way to convey information to your audience. Sometimes, a picture can tell the story better than words ever could. And, graphics have the ability to keep an audience engaged and focused on what you have to say. PowerPoint 2010 gives you the ability to add a variety of graphical content to liven up your presentation.

Graphics and images are effective for illustrating concepts and processes that may be difficult to explain otherwise. The use of photos can help place your audience in a different environment to understand events from around the world. Becoming familiar with the various methods of adding graphical content in PowerPoint will give you a whole new set of options for telling your story and keeping your audience excited about what you have to say.

TOPIC A

Insert Clip Art and Images

You will likely use some types of graphical elements more that others. For example, screen shots from a software application can be helpful in demonstrating how to accomplish a particular task. Also, there are common concepts, such as money or technology, that you will need to discuss. Quick access to commonly used images and the ability to share your computer screen will help you convey information to the audience without filling slide after slide with large amounts of text.

PowerPoint 2010 has a number of built-in graphics features that you can use to make your point. Using on-screen graphics gets your message across quickly to an audience that will, likely, not have a lot of time to review excessive textual content. And, nothing makes a presentation more boring than lengthy, hard-to-read text.

Pictures

Pictures are the most basic form of graphical content you can add to your PowerPoint presentation. Nearly any type of image file that you can store on your hard drive can be inserted into a slide. Selecting the **Picture** button from the **Images** group on the **Insert** tab will launch the **Insert Picture** dialog box. From there, you can navigate to any image you would like to insert into your project.

Clip Art

Clip art is digital graphical content, either in the form of photographs or illustrations, that you can add to your presentation. PowerPoint 2010 can access a clip art repository, containing a variety of images, that you can search for by using key words. The clip art repository also contains movies and sound clips for use in your presentations. If the particular image that you are searching for is not in the clip art repository, you can search thousands of images on Office.microsoft.com.

Figure 4–1: Clip art.

The Clip Art Pane

You can access the clip art repository from the **Clip Art** pane. The **Clip Art** pane provides you with several search options for finding the images, movies, or sounds you are looking for.

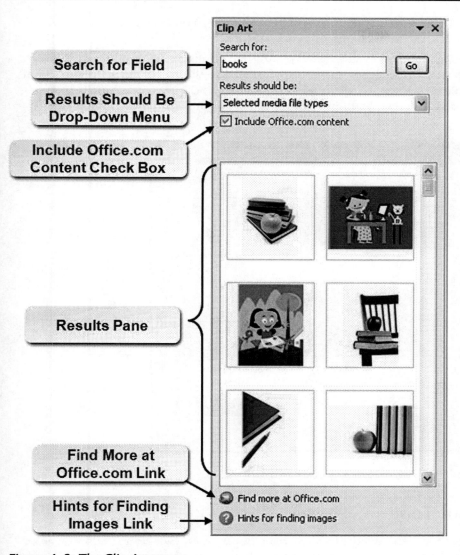

Figure 4–2: The Clip Art pane.

Clip Art Pane Element	Description
Search For field	Allows you to enter key words to search for clip art.
Results Should Be drop-down menu	Filters your results among illustrations, photographs, movies, audio, or all of these media types.
Include Office.com Content check box	Allow you to include or exclude search results from the Office.com website.
Results Pane	Displays your search results.
Find More at Office.com link	Links you to the Office.com website to search for media files not available in the repository.
Hints for Finding Images link	Launches PowerPoint Help and displays Help topics related to using clip art.

The Photo Album Feature

The *photo album feature* allows you to insert and display photographs in a custom presentation that looks like a photo album. PowerPoint 2010 provides you with the capability to add transitions, backgrounds, layouts, themes, and captions to your photo albums. You can also share your photo albums as attachments, as web publications, or in printed form.

The Photo Album dialog box allows you to insert photos into an album, add captions to photos, and modify the photo album layout. You can also apply effects to the images in your photo albums, such as converting images to black and white, adjusting the brightness or contrast, rotating images, and adding frames. You can access the **Photo Album** dialog box in the **Images** group on the **Insert** tab.

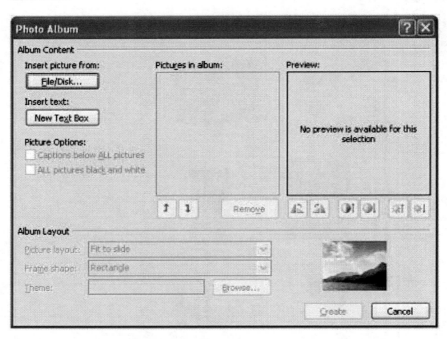

Figure 4–3: The Photo Album dialog box.

The Screenshot Tool

The screenshot tool gives you the ability to add anything displayed on your computer screen as an image in PowerPoint. The **Screenshot** drop-down menu in the **Images** group displays a gallery of windows that are available for capture, and provides you with access to the **Screen Clipping** option. You can insert an image of an entire window, or use the screen clipping option to select a particular region.

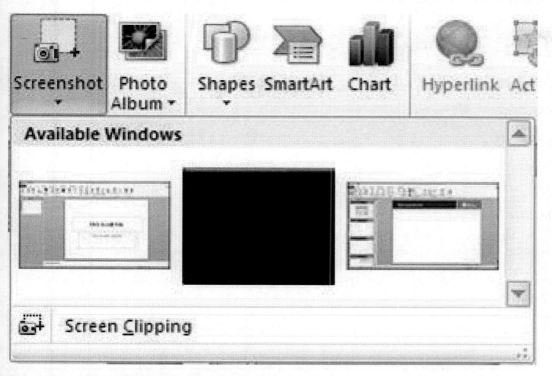

Figure 4-4: The Available Windows dialog box.

 Note: Only windows that are not minimized to the task bar appear in the Available Windows pane. If you wish to insert a screen capture of your desktop, you must use the screen clipping option.

 Note: To further explore the screenshot tool, you can access the LearnTO **Use the PowerPoint Screenshot Tool** presentation from the **LearnTO** tile on the LogicalCHOICE Course screen.

 Access the Checklist tile on your LogicalCHOICE course screen for reference information and job aids on How to Insert Clip Art and Images

ACTIVITY 4-1
Inserting Clip Art and Images

Data Files

Develetech Ind.pptx

videogame_front.png

Scenario

You have completed your orientation and training at Develetech Industries, and you have begun working with one of the product development teams. Each team is developing one product that will be part of Develetech's next seasonal product roll out, New Visions Now. As part of the project kickoff, Develetech is holding a series of internal meetings to introduce the new products to Develetech employees. Members of the various design teams have begun putting together a PowerPoint presentation to introduce the new products. Your supervisor has asked you to add one more image of the video game console your team is developing, and to enhance the title slide with clip art.

---

1. Open the Develetech Ind.pptx file from the C:\091031Data\Adding Graphical Elements to Your Presentation folder.

2. Add clip art to a slide.
   a) Ensure slide 1 is selected in the left pane.
   b) Select **Insert→Images→Clip Art**.
   c) In the **Clip Art** pane, ensure the **Include Office.com content** check box is checked.
   d) Select the **down arrow** in the **Results should be field**, and then ensure that only the **Illustrations** and **Photographs** check boxes are checked.
   e) In the **Search for** field, enter *horizons*, and then select **Go**.
   f) From the search results, select an image of the sun on the horizon.
   g) Select the **Close** button to close the **Clip Art** pane.
   h) Resize the image so that it is small enough to fit below the "New Visions Now" text, and then click and drag the image so that it is centered below the text.

3. Add an image to a slide.
   a) Navigate to slide 12.
   b) From the **Images** group, select **Picture**.
   c) Navigate to the folder C:\091031Data\Adding Graphical Elements to Your Presentation.
   d) Select the videogame_front.png file, and then select **Insert**.
   e) Click and drag the image so that it is centered above the left-most image on the slide.
   f) Click anywhere outside the image to deselect it.

4. Save the presentation as My Develetech Ind.pptx.

TOPIC B

Insert Shapes

Adding existing images and clip art to your presentations is a quick and effective way to illustrate key points to your audience. But you may not always have the right image for your message. You are likely to encounter situations in which it would be best to create your own graphics.

PowerPoint 2010 allows you to add and customize a variety of shapes to your presentations. Shapes can serve as visual cues, adding emphasis to other on-screen elements. You can also use shapes as text boxes, allowing you to create in-depth diagrams or flow charts, and giving you additional options for customizing your textual content.

Shapes

Shapes are common geometric objects that you can add to your PowerPoint presentations. PowerPoint 2010 contains a variety of pre-existing shapes that you can use to build complex figures or illustrations. You can also use shapes as text boxes, giving you further options for customizing the presentation of text in your presentations. Like text boxes, shapes can also contain color, effects, and other style elements. You can access shapes in the **Illustrations** group on the **Insert** tab.

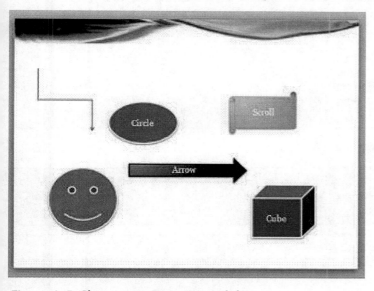

Figure 4–5: Shapes in a PowerPoint slide.

Shape Categories

The available PowerPoint shapes are organized into nine categories: lines, rectangles, basic shapes, block arrows, equation shapes, flow chart, stars and banners, callouts, and action buttons. You can use the shapes from these categories to develop your content in PowerPoint.

Figure 4-6: Some of the shape categories in PowerPoint 2010.

The Drawing Tools Contextual Tab

PowerPoint 2010 provides you with a number of commands for modifying shapes in your presentation. You can access these commands on the **Drawing Tools** contextual tab whenever shapes or text boxes are selected.

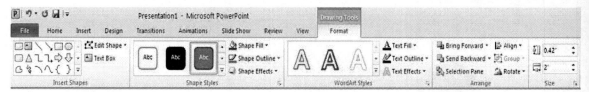

Figure 4-7: The Drawing Tools contextual tab.

 Note: As mentioned in Lesson 3, the commands for modifying shapes are the same as the commands for modifying text boxes. Shapes are, essentially, a more complex version of text boxes.

Drawing Tools Contextual Tab Group	Contains Commands For
Insert Shapes	Inserting or modifying shapes in your presentation.
Shape Styles	Applying various style elements to shapes.
WordArt Styles	Applying various style elements to the text in your shapes.
Arrange	Arranging shapes and other objects on your slides.
Size	Adjusting the size of shapes and other objects on your slides.

 Access the Checklist tile on your LogicalCHOICE course screen for reference information and job aids on How to Insert Shapes

ACTIVITY 4-2
Inserting Shapes

Before You Begin
My Develetech Ind.pptx is open.

Scenario
The new product images and several of the key slides are now in place for the new product presentation. Now, you will need to add product feature information about your team's design to the product slide. You decide to use a shape to display that information.

1. Add a shape to the slide.
   a) Navigate to slide 12.
   b) Select **Insert→Illustrations→Shapes**.
   c) In the **Shapes** gallery, from the **Rectangles** section, select **Rounded Rectangle**, which is the second option.
   d) Click and drag the mouse pointer to draw a rounded rectangle on the right side of the slide.

2. Add text to a shape.
   a) With the shape selected, type *Product Features*.
   b) Select **Home→Paragraph→Align Text**.
   c) Select **Top** from the drop-down menu.

3. Wrap the text to fit the shape.
   a) Ensure the shape is still selected.
   b) Access the **Drawing Tools** contextual tab, and then select the **Shape Styles** section's **dialog box launcher** to display the **Format Shape** dialog box.
   c) Select the **Text Box** tab.
   d) From the **Text Box** pane, in the **Internal margin** section, verify that the **Wrap text in shape** check box is checked.

4. Format the shape.
   a) In the **Format Shape** dialog box, select the **Fill** tab.
   b) In the **Fill** pane, select the **Pattern fill** radio button.
   c) Select the **90%** pattern from the bottom of the second column in the gallery.
   d) Select the **Background Color** button and, in the **Theme Colors** menu, select **Black, Text 1**, which is the second color in the top row.
   e) From the **Format Shape** dialog box, select the **Glow and Soft Edges** tab.
   f) In the **Glow and Soft Edges** pane, in the **Glow** section, select the **Presets** button.
   g) Select **Blue, 18 pt glow, Accent color 1** from the bottom of the first column in the **Glow Variations** gallery.
   h) In the **Glow** section, select the **Color** button and then, in the **Theme Colors** menu, select **Dark Blue, Text 2** from the top of the fourth column.
   i) Select **Close** to close the **Format Shape** gallery.

5. Set the shape formatting as the default shape formatting for the presentation.
   a) If necessary, select the shape.
   b) Right-click the shape, and then select **Set as Default Shape** from the pop-up menu.
   c) Insert a different shape anywhere on the slide.

    d) Verify that the formatting is the same for the new shape, and then delete the shape.

6. Select **File→Save**, and then close the file.

Summary

Your presentation has come a long way since you first created and saved it. You have a dynamic, well organized presentation with text, images, and graphics. Now that you are familiar with how to add a variety of multimedia elements to your presentation, it's time to start focusing on fine-tuning the content on your slides.

Which of the embedded graphical content functions do you think will come in handiest as you create presentations in PowerPoint?

What are some creative and effective ways that you have seen people use graphics in PowerPoint presentations? What kind of impact did they have on you as an audience member?

Note: Check your LogicalCHOICE Course screen for opportunities to interact with your classmates, peers, and the larger LogicalCHOICE online community about the topics covered in this course or other topics you are interested in. From the Course screen you can also access available resources for a more continuous learning experience.

5 | Modifying Objects in Your Presentation

Lesson Time: 1 hour, 15 minutes

Lesson Objectives

In this lesson, you will modify objects in your presentation. You will:

- Edit objects.

- Format objects.

- Group objects.

- Arrange objects.

- Animate objects.

Lesson Introduction

Adding a variety of elements to your presentation is a powerful way to deliver your message and keep your audience interested. But too many objects on screen at once, or objects that don't seem to fit well together, can cause clutter and distract the audience. As you work with a larger variety of multimedia objects, you run the risk of putting too much content on your slides.

The ability to modify and arrange on-screen objects can help you avoid clutter and create slides with a sense of balance and continuity. By utilizing the graphical editing capabilities in PowerPoint 2010, you can avoid the pitfalls of slide clutter and deliver a well-balanced, aesthetically pleasing presentation.

TOPIC A

Edit Objects

Sometimes, objects just don't mesh well together on screen. There might be too much content on a slide. If an image is too big, text may look out of place next to it. Or, you may inadvertently give an object too much emphasis when it is not the focus of your message. You can make simple changes to an on-screen object to fix these problems.

As you include more and more graphical content, you are likely to need to make some adjustments to keep your presentation fresh and pleasing to the eye. PowerPoint has a number of editing features that allow you to tailor your graphics to suit your needs.

Object Selection Methods

To modify an object in your slides, you must first select it. Once you select an object, it becomes active and will be displayed with the border, sizing handles, and rotation handle. PowerPoint 2010 provides you with a number of methods for selecting a single object or multiple objects: selecting screen objects, using keyboard shortcuts, using the **Select** drop-down menu, and using the **Selection Pane**.

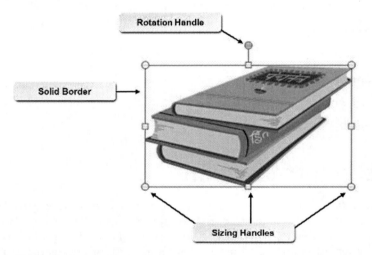

Figure 5–1: A selected image.

 Access the Checklist tile on your LogicalCHOICE course screen for reference information and job aids on How to Select Objects

Image Cropping

You may want to add an image to your presentation that contains some content that you don't want to display. *Cropping* an image allows you to include only the parts of the image that you want. Think of cropping as being similar to cutting a physical photograph with a pair of scissors. You can access the **Crop** command on the **Size** group in the **Picture Tools** contextual tab.

Figure 5-2: An image before and after cropping in PowerPoint.

Picture Tools

It may be necessary to make corrections or adjustments to the images in your presentation. The **Picture Tools** contextual tab provides you with access to PowerPoint's array of picture formatting and correction tools.

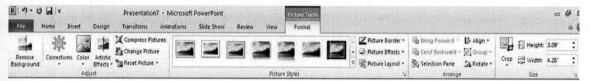

Figure 5-3: The Picture Tools contextual tab.

Picture Tool Functional Group	Provides Commands To
Adjust	Adjust the color, contrast, and brightness of images.
Picture Styles	Format an image's shape, border, or outline, and apply image effects.
Arrange	Position objects on slides relative to other images and text.
Size	Resize, crop, and rotate images.

The Remove Background Feature

The *Remove Background feature* allows you to remove background elements from images, leaving only the subject elements you would like to include from the image. The Remove Background feature will automatically determine what is in the background and what is the main subject of the image. This feature also provides you with certain commands that you can use to select which elements of an image to keep and which to remove. You can access the Remove Background feature on the **Picture Tools** contextual tab in the **Adjust** group.

Figure 5-4: The Background Removal tab provides commands to customize background removal.

Background Removal Command	Function
Mark Areas to Keep	Draws lines to mark areas to keep in the picture.
Mark Areas to Remove	Draws lines to mark areas to remove from the picture.
Delete Mark	Deletes any lines you have drawn either to keep or remove areas of the picture.
Discard All Changes	Closes the **Background Removal** feature without making any changes to the original picture.
Keep Changes	Removes the background, either automatically or according to the lines you have drawn, and closes the **Background Removal** feature.

Object Resizing Methods

Resizing is the process of changing the height and width of an object. You can use the sizing handles to resize a selected object, or you can use the commands on the **Picture Tools** contextual tab in the **Size** group. To adjust the size of an object on your slides, use the **Shape Height** increase/decrease arrows or the **Shape Width** increase/decrease arrows in the **Size** group.

Figure 5-5: The Size group.

Object Scaling Methods

Scaling an object is similar to resizing an object. However, with scaling, you maintain the original ratio of height to width of the object. PowerPoint 2010 provides you with several scaling options in the **Format Picture** dialog box's **Scale** section.

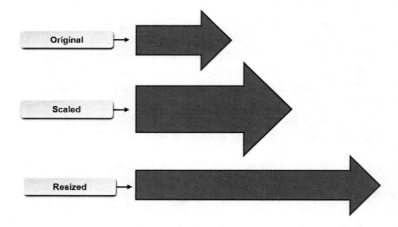

Figure 5-6: Scaling versus resizing.

Scaling Option	Description
Lock Aspect Ratio	Automatically adjusts the height of an object as you adjust its width, and vice versa. This ensures true scaling.

Scaling Option	Description
Relative to Original Picture Size	If you have altered an image's original aspect ratio, this feature will restore the original aspect ratio upon further size adjustments.
Best Scale for Slide Show	Prevents objects such as bitmaps and some movie clips from appearing distorted when presenting a slide show.

 Note: The scaling option check box functions apply only when using the dialog box or ribbon commands. If you resize an object with the diagonal resizing handles, it always scales. If you resize it by using the top, bottom, or side resizing handles, scale is not preserved.

Object Orientation Options

Orientation refers to the angle at which you display the objects on your slides. PowerPoint gives you the ability to rotate objects at any angle and flip objects horizontally and vertically. When an object is selected, you can rotate it either clockwise or counterclockwise using the rotation handle. Pressing and holding the Shift key as you rotate an object rotates it in 15-degree increments.

There are also several orientation commands available on the **Picture Tools** contextual tab, in the **Arrange** group, in the **Rotate** drop-down menu.

Orientation Option	Allows You To
Rotate Right 90°	Rotate an object 1/4 turn to the right.
Rotate Left 90°	Rotate an object 1/4 turn to the left.
Flip Vertical	Flip an object across the vertical plane. This is not the same as rotating an object 180 degrees. This option creates a vertical mirror image of the object.
Flip Horizontal	Flip an object across the horizontal plane to create a mirror image of the original object.
More Rotation Options	Access the **Format Picture** dialog box. From there, you can rotate an object in one-degree increments.

Image Compression Options

Adding a large number of images to your presentation will, naturally, make your presentation's file size large. *Image compression* allows you to reduce the file size of the images in your presentation, reducing the overall size of the presentation file. This can aid the process of storing or sharing your presentation. You can access the **Compress Pictures** dialog box in the **Adjust** group on the **Picture Tools** contextual tab.

PowerPoint 2010 offers you several options for compressing the images in your presentations.

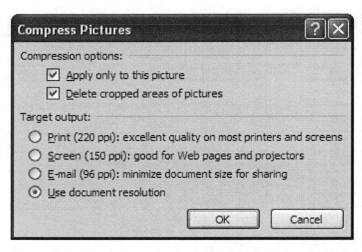

Figure 5–7: Image compression options in the Compress Pictures dialog box.

Compression Option	Description
Apply Only to This Picture	When checked, this option applies compression to only the selected image.
Delete Cropped Areas of Pictures	When checked, this option instructs PowerPoint to delete any part of an image that has been cropped out before compressing images. This further reduces the overall file size.
Print (220 ppi)	Target output resolution for images that is ideal for most printers and screens.
Screen (150 ppi)	Target output resolution for images that is good for web pages and projectors.
E-mail (96 ppi)	Target output resolution for images that is ideal for document sharing.
Use Document Resolution	This option uses the document resolution setting that a user has defined in the project options for a PowerPoint presentation. This option is available in the **Backstage** view by selecting **Options→Advanced**.

 Note: Target output options will be grayed out in the **Compress Pictures** dialog box if the resolution of the original image is less than the particular option. In other words, you cannot increase the resolution of an image.

 Access the Checklist tile on your LogicalCHOICE course screen for reference information and job aids on How to Edit Objects in Your Presentation

ACTIVITY 5-1
Editing Objects in Your Presentation

Data Files

Develetech Ind_shapes added.pptx

new sunset.JPG

Scenario

After reviewing the presentation, you and several other members of your team decide some of the graphics don't quite suit the project. You decide to change the image on the title slide, and remove the background of the image used on the section header slides.

---

1. Open the Develetech Ind_shapes added.pptx file from the C:\091031Data\Modifying Objects in Your Presentation folder.

2. Switch the image on the title slide with another image.
   a) Ensure slide 1 is selected in the left pane.
   b) Right-click the image, and then select **Change Picture** in the pop-up menu to display the **Insert Picture** dialog box.
   c) Navigate to the C:\091031Data\Modifying Objects in Your Presentation folder, select **new sunset.JPG**, and then select **Insert**.

3. Crop the image.
   a) Select **Picture Tools contextual tab→Size→Crop**.
   b) Click and drag the top **cropping handle** to crop out the tree at the top of the image, and then select the **Crop** button again to crop to image.

4. Scale the image to fit the screen.
   a) Ensure the image is still selected.
   b) From the **Size** group, select the **dialog box launcher** to display the **Format Picture** dialog box.
   c) In the **Size** pane's **Scale** section, ensure the **Lock aspect ratio** check box is checked.
   d) In the **Size and rotate** section, use the **Height** field's **spin buttons** to increase the image height to 2 inches, and then select **Close**.
   e) Click and drag the image so that it is centered below the "New Visions Now" text.

5. Add an effect to the image.
   a) Select **Artistic Effects** in the **Adjust** group.
   b) From the **Artistic Effects** gallery, select **Texturizer**, which is the second tile in the fourth row.

6. Remove the background from an image.
   a) Navigate to slide 3.
   b) Select the image, and then access the **Picture Tools** contextual tab.
   c) In the **Adjust** group, select **Remove Background**.
   d) On the **Background Removal** tab, in the **Close** group, select **Keep Changes**.

7. Save the file as *My Develetech Ind_shapes added.pptx*

TOPIC B

Format Objects

You have modified the objects in your presentation. They are now the right size, the correct color, and have the artistic effects you prefer. But they still might not seem quite right. Some images may not be a good fit for themes that you have applied to the presentation. Other images may still look cluttered when viewed next to text, even though they are well proportioned on the slide.

It is often necessary to add formatting to the objects in your presentation to further help offset them from other on-screen elements, and help them fit in with the overall look of your project. By adding object formatting, you will refine your presentation for clarity, and ensure your visual content meshes well with your textual content and overall presentation theme. And here's the good news: formatting objects in your presentations is very much the same as formatting text boxes and shapes, which you have already done.

Object Formatting Options

The **Format Shape** dialog box provides you with a variety of commands you can use to format all of the objects that you add to a presentation. Although there are a good number of similarities among the formatting options available for text boxes, shapes, and other objects (such as images and clip art), there are some differences too. For example, the **Text Box** tab options in the **Format Shape** dialog box are available only if you are formatting a shape or a text box. Likewise, the **Picture Corrections**, **Picture Color**, **Artistic Effects**, and **Crop** tabs are not available for text boxes or shapes. Options appear grayed out if they are not available for a selected object.

Figure 5–8: The Text Box options display grayed out for images.

Fill Options

You can apply fills and other background formatting to images in PowerPoint 2010. However, these will appear only if you have cropped part of the image or applied transparency to some of the image.

The Set Transparent Color Option

The Set Transparent Color option allows you to make one of the colors that are present in an image transparent for the entire image. This option is available the **Picture Tools** tab's **Adjust** section in the **Color** drop-down menu.

Picture Formatting Options

The **Picture Styles** section of the **Picture Tools** contextual tab provides you with access to a variety of pre-configured formatting styles for pictures that you add to your presentations. The picture formatting options include many of the formatting options available for all objects, as well as formatting specific for pictures, such as adding picture frames.

 Note: Clip art and images are both considered pictures in terms of formatting objects.

 Access the Checklist tile on your LogicalCHOICE course screen for reference information and job aids on How to Format Pictures and Objects

ACTIVITY 5-2
Formatting Pictures and Objects

Before You Begin
The My Develetech Ind_shapes added.pptx file is open.

Scenario
You have finished editing the objects in the presentation. You and others on the team feel some of the on-screen objects don't stand out from the background as well as they should. You also think the pattern background in the shapes makes the text difficult to read. You decide to add some formatting to the objects in the presentation to help them stand out and to improve readability.

1. Add formatting to an image.

   a) Navigate to slide 1 in the left pane.
   b) Select the image.
   c) Select **Picture Tools contextual tab→Picture Styles→Picture Border**.
   d) From the **Theme Colors** gallery, select **Dark Blue, Text 2**, which is the fourth tile in the first row.
   e) From the **Picture Styles** group, select **Picture Border** and then select **Weight**.
   f) Select **3 pt** from the secondary menu.
   g) From the **Picture Styles** group, select **Picture Effects** and then select **Shadow** from the drop-down menu.
   h) From the bottom of the **Shadow** gallery, select **Shadow Options** to display the **Format Picture** dialog box.
   i) In the **Shadow** pane, select the **Presets** button and then select **Offset Diagonal Bottom Right**, which is the first tile in the **Outer** section of the gallery.
   j) Drag and slide the **slider** next to the **Transparency** field to set the transparency to 10%.
   k) Use the **Size** field's **spin buttons** to increase the shadow size to 101%.
   l) Select **Close** to close the **Format Picture** dialog box.

2. Add formatting to a shape.
   a) Navigate to slide 4.
   b) Select the shape.
   c) Access the **Drawing Tools** contextual tab and, in the **Shape Styles** group, select the **More** button.
   d) Select **Light 1 Outline, Colored Fill - Blue, Accent 1**, which is the third tile in the second column.

3. Select **File→Save**, and then select **File→Close**.

TOPIC C

Group Objects

Knowing how to add objects to your presentations, and how to format those objects, gives you the ability to create and deliver a presentation that will wow your audience. However, the task of individually formatting all of these objects can be daunting and time consuming. So, how do you make your presentation sparkle while staying on schedule?

PowerPoint 2010 gives you the ability to link together multiple objects within a presentation to make modifying them quick and easy. In addition to saving you time and effort, this can also help you maintain a consistent look to your graphical content throughout your presentation.

The Grouping Feature

The *grouping feature* allows you to link multiple objects together, effectively making them a single object. When you apply formatting to the group, you affect all of the objects within the group. When you select grouped items, they are all displayed within a single border, with sizing handles and a rotation handle for the entire group.

You can still resize, rotate, and apply formatting to individual objects within a group. When a group is selected, select the individual object you would like to format independently. The object will appear with its own border and sizing handles, letting you know that you can resize or format it without affecting the rest of the group.

Figure 5–9: Objects grouped together on a PowerPoint slide.

Access the Checklist tile on your LogicalCHOICE course screen for reference information and job aids on **How to Group and Ungroup Objects**

ACTIVITY 5-3
Grouping Objects

Data Files

Develetech Ind_objects formatted.pptx

Scenario

You notice the product images in the presentation appear a bit small compared to the shapes, and you feel they look a bit flat on screen. You decide to resize the images and apply a 3-D Rotation effect to improve the overall look of the presentation. You realize grouping the images before modifying them will save you time and give you consistent results for all of the objects on each slide.

1. Open the Develetech Ind_objects formatted.pptx file from the C:\091031Data\Modifying Objects in Your Presentation folder.

2. Group the objects on a slide.
   a) Navigate to slide 4.
   b) Select all of the product images.
   c) On the **Picture Tools** contextual tab, select **Arrange→Group**.
   d) Select **Group** from the drop-down menu.
   e) Verify that all of the images are displayed within a single border.

3. Modify the images in the group.
   a) Ensure the group is still selected and that all three images are displayed in a single border.
   b) Access the **Picture Tools** contextual tab.
   c) In the **Size** group, use the **Height** field's **spin buttons** to increase the image height to 7".
   d) Use the **Width** field's **spin buttons** to increase the width to 4".
   e) In the **Picture Styles** group, select **Picture Effects**, and then select **3-D Rotation** from the drop-down menu.
   f) In the **3-D Rotation** gallery, select **Perspective Above**, which is the second tile in the first column of the **Perspective** section.

4. Save the file as *My DeveletechInd_objects formatted.pptx*, and then select **File→Close**.

TOPIC D

Arrange Objects

You have put a lot of effort into adding visually appealing graphical content, editing it, and formatting it. Your presentation has a professional look, and is already well-polished. You can't help but feel, though, that some of the graphics and images look cluttered or chaotic. And some of the more important visual elements of your slides are getting lost among the others. So, what do you do?

PowerPoint provides you with a number of options for arranging the objects in your presentation that can help you balance and distinguish some objects from the others. These options can also help you add depth to your slides, enhancing the visual appeal of your presentation and adding emphasis to graphics that need to carry more weight.

Object Order

Object order defines how objects that overlap appear on your slides in relation to each other. An object on the front layer will appear fully visible, regardless of whether or not it overlaps with other objects. An object on the back layer will be partially or completely hidden behind objects that overlap it. PowerPoint gives you the ability to layer objects on your slides to avoid clutter and assign a level of importance to certain objects over others. You can access the object order commands in the **Picture Tools** contextual tab, in the **Arrange** group.

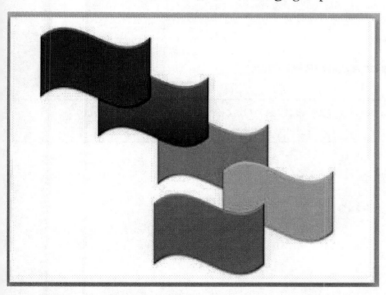

Figure 5-10: Objects on different layers in a PowerPoint slide.

Object Order Option	Moves the Selected Object
Bring Forward	Forward so that it is hidden by fewer objects that are in front of it.
Bring to Front	In front of all other objects so that no part of it is hidden behind another object.
Send Backward	Back so that it is hidden by the objects that are in front of it.
Send to Back	Behind all other objects.

Guides and Gridlines

Guides are lines that allow you to accurately position objects on a slide. The default guides in PowerPoint 2010 appear as a single horizontal line and a single vertical line that intersect at the center of the slides in a presentation. You can add and reposition guides on your slides to suit your needs.

Gridlines are displayed as multiple horizontal and vertical dotted lines, forming a grid on the slides in a presentation. Like guides, gridlines can help you accurately place objects on your slides. Unlike guides, you cannot add or remove gridlines, but you can adjust the spacing between gridlines to suit your needs.

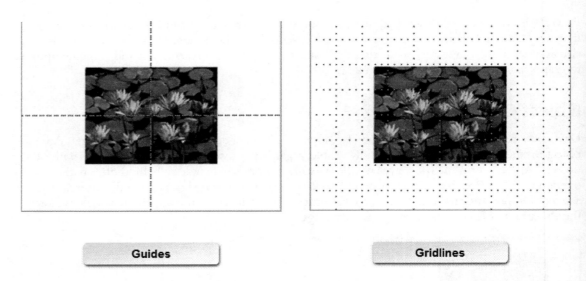

Figure 5-11: Guides and gridlines on a PowerPoint slide.

 Access the Checklist tile on your LogicalCHOICE course screen for reference information and job aids on How to Arrange and Align Objects

ACTIVITY 5-4
Arranging Objects

Data Files

Develetech Ind_objects grouped.pptx

Scenario

You have inserted a slide introducing the new Develetech product names, but your supervisor doesn't like the layout of the shapes on the slide. She has asked you to create a more layered look to the shapes. You decide to arrange and align the shapes on the slide to appear more layered.

1. Open the Develetech Ind_objects grouped.pptx file from the C:\091031Data\Modifying Objects in Your Presentation folder.

2. Use the guides and the gridlines to align the shapes.
   a) Navigate to slide 3.
   b) Access the **View** tab and, in the **Show** group, check the **Gridlines** and the **Guides** check boxes.
   c) Select the three shapes on the left side of the slide.
   d) Access the **Home** tab and then select the **Drawing** group's **dialog box launcher** to display the **Format Shape** dialog box.
   e) Select the **Position** tab, and in the **Position** pane, use the **Horizontal** field's **spin buttons** to align the right side of the selected shapes with the **vertical guide**.
   f) Select **Close** to close the **Format Shape** dialog box.
   g) Select the two shapes on the right side of the slide.
   h) Select the **Drawing** group's **dialog box launcher** to display the **Format Shape** dialog box.
   i) Select the **Position** tab, and then enter *4* into the **Horizontal** field in the **Position** pane.
   j) Select **Close** to close the **Format Shape** dialog box and align the shapes.
   k) Access the **View** tab and, in the **Show** group, uncheck the **Gridlines** and the **Guides** check boxes.

3. Arrange the shapes on the slide.
   a) Select the orange "Knomatico" shape.
   b) Select **Drawing Tools contextual tab→Arrange→Bring Forward down arrow.**
   c) Select **Bring to Front** in the drop-down menu.
   d) Select the blue "Protoi" shape.
   e) In the **Arrange** group, select the **Send Backward down arrow**.
   f) Select **Send Backward** from the drop-down menu.
   g) Repeat sub-steps **e** and **f** as necessary until the blue "Protoi" shape appears behind the light-blue "GeoExis" shape.
   h) Select the green "Handia" shape.
   i) In the **Arrange** group, select the **Send Backward down arrow** and then select **Send to Back** from the drop-down menu.
   j) Click outside the shape to deselect it.

4. Save the file as *My Develetech Ind_objects grouped.pptx*, and then select **File→Close**.

TOPIC E

Animate Objects

Graphics and images can make your presentation look professional, clarify your key points, and add visual appeal for your audience. But too many static images in sequence can begin to look monotonous in a short time. The pictures and shapes that you have so carefully formatted could end up boring the audience, distracting its attention from your message.

Now that you have your visuals fully formatted in place, you will want to consider adding animation to keep your presentation interesting. PowerPoint 2010 gives you the ability to create and customize animation effects that can enhance your presentation and help you further emphasize key points.

Built-in Animation Effects

PowerPoint 2010 contains a wide variety of built-in animation effects that transform your static graphics and text into engaging animations. You can apply animation effects to multiple objects on the same slide, or to a single object. Animations can help you emphasize particular graphical elements, draw your audience to the presentation, and, perhaps, add a bit of humor when appropriate. PowerPoint also provides you with many options for modifying effects. For example, you can change the direction that an object moves or rotates.

Animations are divided into four main categories, with a variety of specific effects in each category. You can access the animation effects in PowerPoint 2010 from the **Animations** tab on the **ribbon**.

 Note: To further explore animations, you can access the LearnTO **Effectively Use PowerPoint Animations and Transitions** presentation from the **LearnTO** tile on the LogicalCHOICE Course screen.

Figure 5-12: The Animation tab.

Animation Category	Use These To
Entrance	Move objects into frame or fade them in.
Emphasis	Draw the audience's attention to a particular object.
Exit	Move objects out of frame or fade them out.
Motion Paths	Generate on-screen motion for particular objects.

The Animation Painter Feature

The *Animation Painter* feature allows you to reapply animation effects to multiple objects. This feature works much like the Format Painter does for text formatting, only for animation. Double-clicking the **Animation Painter** button puts the mouse pointer in **Sticky Mode**, which allows you to keep applying the same animation effect to multiple objects within your presentation, and in other presentations.

 Access the Checklist tile on your LogicalCHOICE course screen for reference information and job aids on How to Animate Objects

ACTIVITY 5-5
Animating Objects

Data Files

Develetech Ind_objects arranged.pptx

Scenario

You are pleased with the new alignment and the new arrangement of the shapes on slide 3 of your presentation. However, because the new product line announcement is such a big event, you feel the slide should be more exciting. You decide to use animation to add energy to the slide.

1. Open the Develetech Ind_objects arranged.pptx file from the C:\091031Data\Modifying Objects in Your Presentation folder.

2. Apply an animation effect to the shapes.
   a) Navigate to slide 3.
   b) Select the orange "Knomatico" shape, and then access the **Animations** tab.
   c) In the **Animation** group, select the **More** button ⊟ to display the **Animation** gallery.
   d) In the **Animation** gallery, in the **Entrance** section, select **Grow & Turn**.
   e) Select the orange "Knomatico" shape, and then select **Effect Options** in the **Animation** group.
   f) Select **By Paragraph** in the drop-down menu.

3. Use the Animation Painter.
   a) Ensure the orange "Knomatico" shape is selected, and then select **Animation Painter** from the **Advanced Animation** group.
   b) Select the red "Melius" shape to apply the animation.

4. Use Sticky Mode to apply the animation to multiple shapes.
   a) Ensure the red "Melius" shape is selected, and then double-click **Animation Painter** in the **Advanced Animation** group.
   b) Select the remaining shapes in turn to apply the animation effect to each.
   c) Click outside the slide to deactivate Sticky Mode.

5. Select **Preview** in the **Preview** group to view the animation.

6. Save the file as *My Develetech_objects arranged.pptx*, and then select **File→Close**.

Summary

You have created a true multimedia presentation, complete with succinct text, engaging graphics, and dynamic animations. Your audience is sure to appreciate and enjoy the presentation. More importantly, the audience will be able pick out and focus on the important points within your message as you have prominently placed and emphasized them on your slides. Your presentation is nearly, but not quite, complete. There are likely to be occasions when you need to present large amounts of complex data within your presentations. Rather than fill your slides with a lot of text or complex graphics, you can present data and other information in table form.

Which of the object-formatting options available in PowerPoint 2010 do you think will save you the most time while helping you create high-impact presentations?

In your experience, how does the addition of animations to presentation graphics enhance the overall experience of viewing the presentation? Are there situations in which animations would not be appropriate?

Note: Check your LogicalCHOICE Course screen for opportunities to interact with your classmates, peers, and the larger LogicalCHOICE online community about the topics covered in this course or other topics you are interested in. From the Course screen you can also access available resources for a more continuous learning experience.

6 Adding Tables to Your Presentation

Lesson Time: 20 minutes

Lesson Objectives

In this lesson, you will add tables to your presentation. You will:

- Create a table.

- Format a table.

- Insert a table from other Microsoft applications.

Lesson Introduction

People commonly use PowerPoint 2010 to create presentations for work meetings and other business-related purposes. It is likely that you will give a presentation that will contain sales figures, budgetary information, or other financial data. Or, perhaps you will need to give a presentation containing scientific data related to a study. When tasked with presenting financial information and other data in a presentation, you will need a way to display the information to the audience without endless slides of figure-dense content.

PowerPoint 2010 gives you the ability to easily add, populate, and work with tables in your presentations. Using tables is an effective way to convey large volumes of numerical content to your audience in an easy-to-digest format.

TOPIC A

Create a Table

Your presentation is nearly complete, and you are happy with the progress you have made. You have honed your message, and your text, graphics, and animation are all in place. You are confident that you can deliver a high-impact, engaging presentation to the audience. Now, you need only include financial and statistical data to your presentation to support your key points.

Numerical data is difficult to present to an audience through text and images alone. Without organizing such data into an easily read or easily interpreted format, your audience will likely miss key information and become frustrated trying to follow the presentation. Using the table features in PowerPoint 2010 can help you present data to your audience in a clear, concise manner.

Tables

Tables are containers for numerical data and other content that are organized into columns and rows of individual *cells*. Tables can range from simple objects with just a few cells, to large, complex objects that contain massive amounts of content. You can format tables with a variety of borders, effects, and styles.

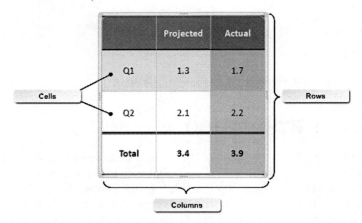

Figure 6–1: A table in PowerPoint.

Table Creation Options

PowerPoint 2010 provides you with several options for creating tables in your presentation. You can create a table by graphically selecting the desired number of columns and rows in the **Insert Table** drop-down menu. You can numerically select the number of columns and rows by using the **Insert Table** dialog box. PowerPoint 2010 also enables you to draw a custom table.

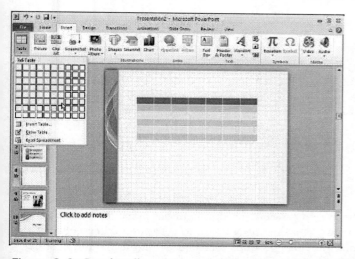

Figure 6-2: Graphically creating a table with the Insert Table drop-down menu.

The Insert Table Dialog Box

The **Insert Table** dialog box enables you to create tables by using spin boxes to select the number of rows and columns you desire.

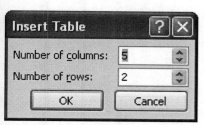

Figure 6-3: The Insert Table dialog box.

Table Navigation Methods

You have several options for navigating the cells in your tables. Navigating from cell to cell allows you to enter data and other information where you need it. You can activate a cell by selecting it with the mouse pointer, or you can navigate from cell to cell by using the keyboard. Once you have selected a cell, you can use the keyboard to enter textual content.

Action	Keystroke
Move one cell to the right	**Tab** or the **Right Arrow** key
Move one cell to the left	**Shift+Tab** or the **Left Arrow** key
Move down one cell	**Down Arrow** key
Move up one cell	**Up Arrow** key

 Access the Checklist tile on your LogicalCHOICE course screen for reference information and job aids on How to Create a Table

ACTIVITY 6-1
Creating a Table

Data Files

Develetech Ind_objects animated.pptx

Scenario

Your supervisor has informed you that the VP of product development has asked that sales projections for the new product line be included in the presentation to generate excitement over the launch. You decide to add a table to display previous product sales figures next to the projections for the new product line.

1. Open the Develetech Ind_objects animated.pptx file from the C:\091031Data\Adding Tables to Your Presentation folder.

2. Create a new slide for the table.
   a) Navigate to slide 13, and then insert a new Title Only slide from the **New Slide** drop-down menu in the **Slides** group.
   b) Enter *Sales Projections* into the title text placeholder.
   c) Use the **Format Painter** to apply the text formatting from the title text on slide 1 to the title text you entered on slide 14.
   d) Click outside the title text placeholder to deselect it.

3. Insert a table on the slide.
   a) Select **Insert→Tables→Table**.
   b) Graphically select a table consisting of four columns and six rows from the **Table** drop-down menu.
   c) Enter the following text into the cells in the first row of the table: *Product, Previous Version Sales $M, Projected Sales $M,* and *Over/Under %*
   d) Enter the new product names in the first column of the table in the following order: *Knomatico, GeoExis, Handia, Melius,* and *Protoi*

4. Save the file as *My Develetech Ind_objects animated.pptx*, and then select **File→Close**.

TOPIC B

Format a Table

You have created the tables you need for your presentation, and you have entered all of the data you need to convey to the audience. But tables can be a bit tricky to read, especially tables that have long columns of numerical figures. You will want to enhance your tables to make them easier for the audience to read. You will also want to make your tables mesh well with the rest of your presentation. Unformatted tables look dull, and they may not blend well with other elements of a presentation that is highly stylized.

PowerPoint 2010 gives you a wide range of options for formatting the tables in your presentations. You can use the table formatting options to enhance the clarity and the visual appeal of your tables. You can also add graphical elements to your tables, rather than relying solely on figures and other textual content.

The Table Tools Contextual Tab

When you create a table in PowerPoint 2010, the **Table Tools** contextual tab is displayed automatically. The **Table Tools** contextual tab is divided between the **Design** and the **Layout** tabs. These tabs contain all of the commands associated with formatting and modifying the layout of tables.

Figure 6-4: The Table Tools contextual tab.

The Design Tab

The **Design** tab in the **Table Tools** contextual tab gives you access to the various commands you will use to format the overall look of your tables.

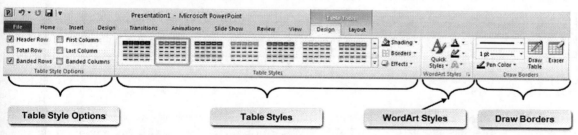

Figure 6-5: The functional groups on the Design tab.

Functional Group	Provides Commands For
Table Style Options	Highlighting particular areas of your tables to enhance clarity. For example, alternate rows or columns can be shaded different colors to make the table easier to read.
Table Styles	Formatting the overall look of your tables. Use the commands in the **Table Styles** group to add shading to cells, modify the look of borders, or apply graphical effects to your tables.

Functional Group	Provides Commands For
WordArt Styles	Adding and modifying WordArt.
Draw Borders	Drawing in or erasing columns and rows.

The Layout Tab

The **Layout** tab in the **Table Tools** contextual tab gives you access to the various commands you will use to format the structure of your tables.

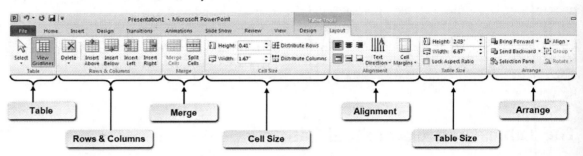

Figure 6-6: The functional groups on the Layout tab.

Functional Group	Provides Commands For
Table	Displaying the gridlines within tables and selecting areas of tables for formatting.
Rows & Columns	Adding or deleting rows and columns.
Merge	Merging or splitting cells.
Cell Size	Modifying the size of cells in a table.
Alignment	Aligning the text within cells.
Table Size	Modifying the size of the table.
Arrange	Arranging graphical objects within cells, and arranging the table in relation to other objects.

 Note: Arranging objects is covered in depth in Lesson 5.

Table Styles

As with many other features in PowerPoint 2010, you can quickly apply pre-formatted styles to your tables. The **Table Styles** gallery in the **Table Styles** group provides you with an array of quick styles that you can apply to the tables in your presentations.

Figure 6-7: The Table Styles gallery.

Table Fill Options

As with other objects in your presentation, PowerPoint 2010 gives you the ability to customize the backgrounds of cells and tables. You can access the commands to apply various fills to your tables by accessing the **Shading** drop-down menu in the **Table Styles** group. In addition to solid color backgrounds, gradient, texture, and picture fills are available in cells and tables.

 Note: Formatting fills is covered in depth in Lessons 2 and 3.

 Access the Checklist tile on your LogicalCHOICE course screen for reference information and job aids on How to Format a Table

ACTIVITY 6-2
Formatting a Table

Data Files

Develetech Ind_table inserted.pptx

Scenario

You have added the sales figures to the table in the presentation. As the table is fairly small relative to the slide, you decide to scale up the table to better fill the slide. You also decide that the table does not blend well visually with other objects throughout the presentation. You decide to format the table to better suit the presentation.

1. Open the Develetech Ind_table inserted.pptx file from the C:\091031Data\Adding Tables to Your Presentation folder.

2. Resize and align the table to fit the slide.
   a) Navigate to slide 14, and then select the table.
   b) Within the **Table Tools** contextual tab, access the **Layout** tab.
   c) In the **Table Size** group, check the **Lock Aspect Ratio** check box.
   d) Use the **Height** field's **spin buttons** to increase the height of the table to 5".
   e) Access the **View** tab and, in the **Show** group, check the **Guides** check box.
   f) Hover the mouse pointer over the table border until it appears with the **Move** cursor ⬍, and then click and drag the table so that it is centered below the title text on the slide.
   g) In the **Show** group, uncheck the **Guides** check box.

3. Add formatting to the table.
   a) Select the table and, within the **Table Tools** contextual tab, access the **Design** tab.
   b) Select the **More** button ⬇ in the **Table Styles** group and, in the **Table Styles** gallery, select **Light Style 3 - Accent 6**, which is the bottom tile in the last column of the **Light** section.
   c) Select the top row within the table by selecting the "Product" cell, pressing and holding down the **Shift** key, and selecting the "Over/Under %" cell.
   d) Within the **Table Tools** contextual tab, access the **Layout** tab.
   e) In the **Alignment** group, select the **Center** and the **Center Vertically** buttons to center the column title text within the cells.

   f) Click outside the table to deselect it.

4. Save the file as *My Develetech Ind_table inserted.pptx*, and then select **File→Close**.

TOPIC C

Insert a Table from Other Microsoft Office Applications

You can now create tables within your presentations to clearly display figures and other textual information. However, entering numbers into large tables can be a tedious, time-consuming process. And copying large amounts of data manually can lead to mistakes. In such a situation, you will often already have the tables you need for your presentations in other documents. Recreating that work is simply a waste of time.

PowerPoint 2010 gives you the ability to import tables from Microsoft Word and Excel into your presentations. By importing existing tables, you are saving development effort and reducing the potential for errors. This option also facilitates a consistent look and feel across documentation for large projects.

Linking vs. Embedding

There are two methods for importing objects from other files in PowerPoint: *linking* and *embedding*. The main difference between a linked object and an embedded object is where the data is stored. When you link an object to a slide in your presentation, the data is stored in the source file. When the object is updated in the source file, the changes will reflect in your presentation. Linking objects is a good option when another person is responsible for updating the document and you want the changes reflected in your presentation, and when file size is a concern.

When you embed an object in your presentation, your are placing a copy of the data in the PowerPoint file. The object becomes a part of your presentation file and no longer has a connection to the source file. Changes in the source file will not be reflected in your presentation.

The Insert Object Dialog Box

The Insert Object dialog box allows you to insert an object from another file into your presentation. You can choose to create the object in a new file by choosing an application from the **Object Type** field, or to browse your computer for a file from which to insert an object. You can also indicate if you are linking or embedding the object by using the **Link** check box.

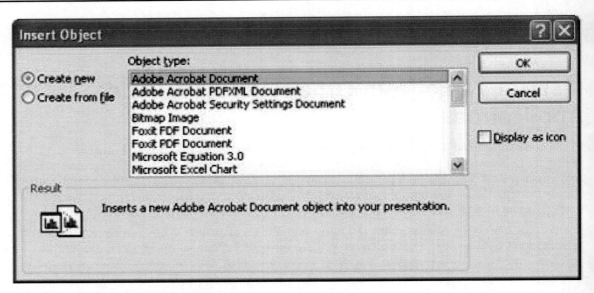

Figure 6-8: The Insert Object dialog box.

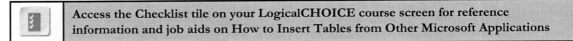

Access the Checklist tile on your LogicalCHOICE course screen for reference information and job aids on How to Insert Tables from Other Microsoft Applications

ACTIVITY 6-3
Inserting a Microsoft Excel Spreadsheet

Data Files

Develetech Ind_table formatted.pptx

New Visions Now Contacts.xlsx

Before You Begin

Microsoft Excel® 2010 is installed.

Scenario

As the presentation is nearly ready for delivery, you have asked several people to review the content. You have received multiple requests from the reviewers to include a list of important contacts for the project teams associated with the various new projects. Another member of your development team has an existing Microsoft Excel spreadsheet with all of the contacts. You ask him to send it to you so you can include it in the presentation. You decide to link the Excel file to the presentation so any future changes will need to be made in only one document.

1. Open the Develetech Ind_table formatted.pptx file from the C:\091031Data\Adding Tables to Your Presentation folder.

2. Create a new slide for the spreadsheet.
   a) Navigate to slide 14 and, in the **Slides** group's **New Slides** drop-down menu, insert a new Title Only slide.
   b) Enter *Who's Who?* in the title text placeholder.
   c) Use the **Format Painter** to apply the text formatting from the title text on slide 14 to the title text you entered on slide 15.
   d) Click outside the title text placeholder to deselect it.

3. Link the Excel spreadsheet to the slide.
   a) Select **Insert→Text→Object** to display the **Insert Object** dialog box.
   b) Select the **Create from file** radio button, and then select **Browse** to display the **Browse** dialog box.
   c) Navigate to the C:\091031Data\Adding Tables to Your Presentation folder.
   d) Select New Visions Now Contacts.xlsx and then select **OK**.
   e) Check the **Link** check box, and then select **OK** in the **Insert Object** dialog box.

4. Apply formatting to the new table.
   a) Select the table, and then access the **Drawing Tools** contextual tab.
   b) In the **Shape Styles** group, select **Shape Fill** and then select **Orange, Accent 6**, which is the last tile in the first row of the **Theme Colors** drop-down menu.

5. Save the file as *My Develetech Ind_table formatted.pptx*, and then select **File→Close**.

Summary

You have added tables to your presentation to convey large amounts of numerical data to your audience. Your tables are formatted so that they are easy to read and fit well with the overall look of your presentation. Although this is certainly preferable to multiple slides of dense textual content, some large tables are still difficult to read and interpret. You need a way for the audience to analyze the information you are presenting quickly and easily. Now that you have all of the necessary data in your presentation, you are ready to transform that data into easy-to-read charts.

What are some creative uses for tables that you will be able to include in a variety of presentations?

What advantages, not already discussed, are there to using existing tables and spreadsheets in presentations?

 Note: Check your LogicalCHOICE Course screen for opportunities to interact with your classmates, peers, and the larger LogicalCHOICE online community about the topics covered in this course or other topics you are interested in. From the Course screen you can also access available resources for a more continuous learning experience.

7 | Adding Charts to Your Presentation

Lesson Time: 35 minutes

Lesson Objectives

In this lesson, you will add charts to your presentation. You will:

- Create a chart.
- Format a chart.
- Insert a chart from Microsoft Excel.

Lesson Introduction

It is sometimes difficult for an audience to digest large amounts of data or financial information by glancing over tables. This is especially true for long tables that have many columns. In larger rooms, it may be difficult for some audience members to see such figures on the screen. You typically don't have the time available for people to spend analyzing complex tables. And, quite frankly, that can make for a boring presentation. You need a way to quickly show the audience members why all of this information matters to them.

Microsoft® Office PowerPoint® provides you with the ability to create eye-catching charts that show the meaning behind complex strings of data. You have a vast array of options for formatting these charts to make your point clearly, and to show the audience a broader view of the data. Using these features lends visual appeal to your presentations and reduces the amount of time you need to spend explaining complex numerical relationships.

TOPIC A

Create a Chart

You have added tables to your presentation, and these tables contain information about sales trends, research findings, or other key matters. To most of the audience, all that matters is the impact of this information. You may need to convert the data in your tables into charts that your audience can analyze and interpret on the spot.

Charts help you visually represent numerical information to your audience. You can create a variety of charts in PowerPoint 2010, allowing you to tailor charts to best suit the specific needs of your presentation.

Charts

Charts are graphical representations of numerical or mathematical data. You can use charts to display the relationships among groups of numbers from spreadsheets and tables. In PowerPoint 2010, charts may also contain titles, legends, and a data table.

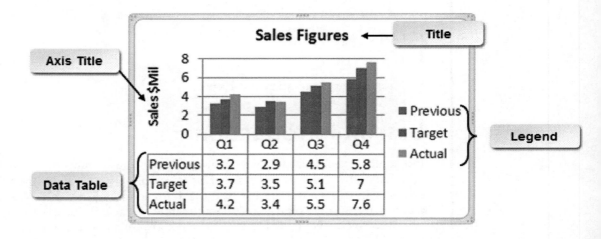

Figure 7–1: A typical column chart in PowerPoint 2010.

Chart Data

When you insert a chart into your presentation, PowerPoint automatically launches a Microsoft® Excel® worksheet in a separate window containing sample data that will populate the chart. The sample data worksheet contains labels for the columns and rows. These labels appear in a preview of the chart on the slide. You can change the labels and the data to suit your needs. You can also add rows or columns to the worksheet. The chart automatically reflects the changes as you make them. Although the worksheet opens in Excel, there is no separate Excel file. The data for the chart is contained within, and saved along with, the PowerPoint file.

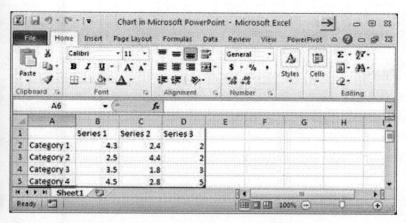

Figure 7–2: Sample data in an Excel worksheet.

The Switch Row/Column Feature

You can switch the rows and the columns of chart data between axes by using the *Switch Row/ Column* feature. This feature allows you change the orientation of information along the X and the Y axes without having to re-enter your data. The data that is charted along the X axis becomes the data charted along the Y axis and vice versa. You can find this feature by selecting **Chart Tools→Design**.

 Note: The **Switch Row/Column** feature is disabled when the Excel worksheet containing the chart data is closed.

Chart Types

PowerPoint 2010 offers you 11 types of charts for you to use in your presentations. The type of chart you use will depend on the type of information you wish to convey, as each is well suited to particular uses. Each of the 11 chart types contains a gallery of chart subtypes. When you insert a chart into your presentation, the **Insert Chart** dialog box displays, allowing you to select the best chart subtype for your presentation. The table following the figure describes some of the more commonly used chart types.

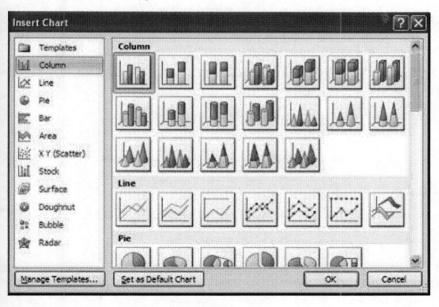

Figure 7–3: The Insert Chart dialog box.

Chart Type	Is Used for Plotting Data
Column	That is arranged in columns and rows in tables and spreadsheets. Column charts are useful for plotting data changes over time, and for making comparisons. Column charts typically contain categories along the X axis, and numerical figures along the Y axis.
Line	That is arranged in columns and rows in tables and spreadsheets. Line charts are ideal for illustrating trends over time.
Pie	From a single column or row. Pie charts are useful for displaying values as a percentage of the whole.
Bar	That is arranged in columns and rows. Bar charts are best suited to making comparisons among items.

 Access the Checklist tile on your LogicalCHOICE course screen for reference information and job aids on How to Create a Chart

ACTIVITY 7-1
Creating a Chart

Data Files
Develetech Ind_spreadsheet added.pptx

Scenario
You decide that a visual representation of the projected sales growth for the new product line would make a big impact on Develetech employees at the product launch meetings. You decide to use a chart to visually demonstrate the company's projected sales increases due to the new product rollouts.

---

1. Open the Develetech Ind_spreadsheet added.pptx file from the C:\091031Data\Adding Charts to Your Presentation folder. When prompted, in the **Microsoft PowerPoint Security Notice** dialog box, select **Update Links**.

2. Insert a chart into the presentation.
   a) Navigate to slide 14, and then insert a new **Blank** slide from the **New Slides** drop-down menu in the **Slides** group.
   b) Select **Insert→Illustrations→Chart**.
   c) From the **Insert Chart** dialog box, select **Clustered Column**, which is the first tile in the **Column** section of the **Chart** gallery.
   d) Select **OK** to create the chart.

3. Edit the chart data.
   a) In the Excel worksheet, click the lower right corner of the range, and then drag it so that it outlines an area of the worksheet that has 5 series and 2 categories.

◢	A	B	C	D	E	F
1		Series 1	Series 2	Series 3	Series 4	Series 5
2	Category 1	4.3	2.4	2		
3	Category 2	2.5	4.4	2		

   b) Delete the data outside the range by selecting the cells and pressing the **Delete** key.
   c) Select cell **B1**, and then type *Knomatico* into the cell.
   d) Select cell **C1** and type *GeoExis*, select cell **D1** and type *Handia*, select cell **E1** and type *Melius*, and then select cell **F1** and type *Protoi*.
   e) Select cell **A2** and type *Previous Version Sales $M*, and then select cell **A3** and type *Projected Sales $M*
   f) Enter the numerical data from the image below into the remaining cells in the Excel worksheet.

◢	A	B	C	D	E	F
1		Knomatico	GeoExis	Handia	Melius	Protoi
2	Previous Ve	121.2	345.7	98.6	203.1	78.2
3	Projected Sa	218.1	473.6	110.4	221.4	87.6

   g) Select **File→Close** on the worksheet.

        h) Verify that the changes are reflected in the chart.

4.   Save the file as ***My Develetech Ind_spreadsheet added.pptx***

TOPIC B

Format a Chart

Your presentation now contains charts to graphically display information from your tables and spreadsheets. But you may not have selected the best chart type or chart subtype to convey that information to the audience. Or, you may feel the charts need some tweaking to make certain key points stand out.

PowerPoint 2010 provides you with a host of options for formatting the charts in your presentations. You can also save chart formatting as a template for creating future charts. Becoming more adept at customizing your charts will give you the ability to create simple, clean charts to illustrate even the most complex of numerical relationships.

The Chart Tools Contextual Tab

The **Chart Tools** contextual tab contains all of the commands you will use to create and format your charts. This contextual tab is displayed when you select a chart in a presentation, and it is divided into three tabs: the **Design** tab, the **Layout** tab, and the **Format** tab.

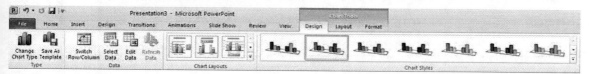

Figure 7–4: The Chart Tools contextual tab.

The Design Tab

The **Design** tab in the **Chart Tools** contextual tab contains the commands you will use to modify the overall style of your charts, and to edit the chart data.

Functional Group	Provides Commands For
Type	Changing the chart type of a chart in your presentation, and for saving a chart as a template.
Data	Editing the chart data.
Chart Layouts	Selecting various chart layouts. The layout of a chart determines which elements, such as titles, legends, and labels, appear on the chart.
Chart Styles	Applying style elements, such as colors, backgrounds, and effects, to your charts.

The Layout Tab

The **Layout** tab in the **Chart Tools** contextual tab contains the commands you will use to add and modify chart elements, and format background elements in your charts.

Functional Group	Provides Commands For
Current Selection	Formatting the selected chart element. The **Current Selection** group also indicates the element of the table that is currently selected.
Insert	Inserting pictures, shapes, and text boxes.

Functional Group	Provides Commands For
Labels	Adding, removing, and formatting labels.
Axes	Modifying axis formating and switching gridlines on and off.
Background	Adding and modifying background formatting of charts. You can also format the floor and the wall when you have selected a 3-D chart style.
Analysis	Adding and removing graphical elements that help analyze the chart.

The Format Tab

The **Format** tab in the **Chart Tools** contextual tab contains the commands you will use to change the appearance of objects on your charts.

Functional Group	Provides Commands For
Current Selection	Formatting the selected object. The **Current Selection** group also indicates the object that is currently selected.
Shape Styles	Applying style elements to objects in your charts.
WordArt Styles	Applying WordArt styles to chart text, such as labels and titles.
Arrange	Arranging and aligning objects on your charts.
Size	Resizing objects on your charts.

Chart Layouts

Chart Layouts are pre-formatted layout options that you can apply to the various chart types in PowerPoint. Chart layouts determine which chart elements, such as labels, titles, and legends, will appear, and where they appear on your charts. PowerPoint also gives you the ability to customize chart layouts by formatting individual chart elements. You can access the **Chart Layouts** gallery from the **Design** tab in the **Chart Tools** contextual tab.

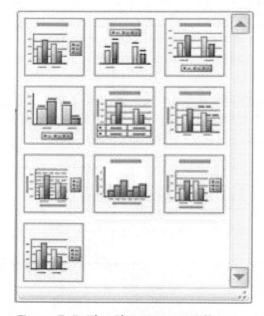

Figure 7–5: The Chart Layout gallery.

Chart Styles

Chart Styles are quick styles that you can apply to charts. Chart styles determine the color of objects and backgrounds, and may contain effects. PowerPoint also gives you the ability to customize chart styles by applying style elements to objects and backgrounds individually. You can access the **Chart Styles** gallery from the **Design** tab in the **Chart Tools** contextual tab.

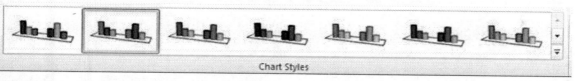

Figure 7-6: The Chart Styles gallery.

 Access the Checklist tile on your LogicalCHOICE course screen for reference information and job aids on How to Format a Chart

ACTIVITY 7–2
Formatting a Chart

Before You Begin
The My Develetech Ind_spreadsheet added.pptx file is open.

Scenario
After adding the chart to the presentation, you decide you don't like the type of chart you selected. You feel it looks too flat on the slide, and so you decide to change the type of chart to one of the 3-D chart types and add some formatting. You also notice there is no title on the chart, so you realize you will need to add one.

1. Change the chart to another chart type.
   a) Ensure slide 15 is selected in the left pane.
   b) Select the chart and, within the **Chart Tools** contextual tab, select the **Design** tab.
   c) In the **Type** group, select **Change Chart Type** to display the **Change Chart Type** dialog box.
   d) In the **Column** section of the **Change Chart Type** dialog box, select **3-D Clustered Column**, which is the fourth tile in the first row, and then select **OK**.
   e) Verify that the chart type has changed.

2. Modify the layout of the chart.
   a) Within the **Chart Tools** contextual tab, access the **Layout** tab.
   b) In the **Labels** group, select **Chart Title** and then select **Above Chart** from the drop-down menu.
   c) Type *Sales Projections* in the title text box.
   d) Click outside the text box to deselect it.
   e) If necessary, select the chart.
   f) From the **Labels** group, select **Legend** and then select **Show Legend at Left** from the drop-down menu.
   g) From the **Axes** group, select **Gridlines** and then select **Primary Horizontal Gridlines** from the drop-down menu.
   h) Select **Major & Minor Gridlines** from the secondary menu.

3. Add formatting to the chart.
   a) Within the **Chart Tools** contextual tab, access the **Design** tab.
   b) In the **Chart Styles** section, select the **More** button ⬇ , and then select **Style 8**, which is the last tile in the top row of the **Chart Styles** gallery.
   c) Within the **Chart Tools** contextual tab, access the **Format** tab and then, from the **Current Selection** group's drop-down menu, select **Back Wall**.
   d) From the **Current Selection** group, select **Format Selection** to display the **Format Wall** dialog box.
   e) Select the **Gradient fill** radio button.
   f) Select the **Color** button, and then select **Orange, Accent 6, Lighter 80%**, which is the second tile in the last column of the **Theme Colors** menu.
   g) Select **Close**.
   h) From the **Current Selection** group's drop-down menu, select **Side Wall** and then select **Format Selection** to display the **Format Wall** dialog box.
   i) Select the **Gradient Fill** radio button, and then select **Close**.
   j) From the **Current Selection** group's drop-down menu, select **Chart Area** and then select **Format Selection** to display the **Format Chart Area** dialog box.

k) Select the **Position** tab.

l) From the **Position on Slide** section of the **Position** pane, use the **Vertical** field's **spin buttons** to increase the vertical distance of the chart to 1.8" from the top left corner of the slide.

m) Select **Close**.

4. Select **File→Save**.

TOPIC C

Insert a Chart from Microsoft Excel

You can now create a vast array of charts to quickly illustrate the meaning behind large amounts of numerical data. While there are clear benefits to utilizing the chart functionality in PowerPoint 2010, as with tables, there is no point in duplicating work you have already performed. Let's face it, it takes time to create, populate, and format a chart that will make an impact. If you have created one already, there is no need to spend the time doing it again.

PowerPoint 2010 lets you insert existing Microsoft Excel charts to your presentations. Linking existing charts to your PowerPoint presentations offers the same benefits as using existing tables. You will save time and effort, avoid data errors, and facilitate a consistent look across various documents.

 Access the Checklist tile on your LogicalCHOICE course screen for reference information and job aids on **How to Insert a Chart from Microsoft Excel**

ACTIVITY 7–3
Inserting a Chart From Microsoft Excel

Data Files

Develetech Ind_chart formatted.pptx

Develetech market share.xlsx

Before You Begin

The My Develetech Ind_spreadsheet added.pptx file is open.

Scenario

You have received an additional request from the VP of product development. He has asked your supervisor to have you include two existing pie charts that he put together. The charts show Develetech's market share from the previous product line, and the projected company market share from the new product rollout. You decide to link the charts to the presentation so that any changes to the projections can be easily reflected in the presentation.

---

1. Insert two new slides for the pie charts.
   a) Navigate to slide 15.
   b) On the **Home** tab, from the **Slides** group's **New Slide** drop-down menu, insert two new Blank slides.

2. In Excel, open the **Develetech market share.xlsx** file from the C:\091031Data\Adding Charts to Your Presentation folder.

3. Link the existing charts to the presentation.
   a) Select the **Previous Market Share** chart and, in the **Clipboard** group, select the **Copy** button.
   b) Switch back to the presentation, and then navigate to slide 16.
   c) From the **Home** tab, in the **Clipboard** group, select the **Paste down-arrow** and then select **Use Destination Theme & Link Data** 🖼 from the drop-down menu.
   d) Navigate to slide 17.
   e) Switch to the Develetech market share.xlsx file.
   f) Scroll down and select the **Projected Market Share** chart, and then copy it to the clipboard.
   g) Switch back to the presentation.
   h) From the **Paste Options** drop-down menu, link the chart to the slide by selecting **Use Destination Theme & Link Data**.
   i) Close the Excel 2010 application.

4. In the presentation, select **File→Save**, and then select **File→Close**.

Summary

Your PowerPoint presentation is now complete! You have developed a truly engaging multimedia presentation that will help you deliver your message and make a big impact on the audience. It is important to note, however, that your PowerPoint file is not the actual presentation. Just as a script is different from the actual play, the presentation doesn't occur until you are in front of a live audience making your thoughts, text, and graphics come to life. Now that you have all of your content in place and ready to go, all that's left is a bit of polishing, and preparing for the big event.

In your daily life, where do you most often encounter charts that are being used to make sense of numerical information? Why are they used in these instances?

Which do you think you will use in your presentations more, charts or tables? Why?

 Note: Check your LogicalCHOICE Course screen for opportunities to interact with your classmates, peers, and the larger LogicalCHOICE online community about the topics covered in this course or other topics you are interested in. From the Course screen you can also access available resources for a more continuous learning experience.

8 | Preparing to Deliver Your Presentation

Lesson Time: 40 minutes

Lesson Objectives

In this lesson, you will prepare to deliver your presentation. You will:

- Review your presentation.
- Apply transitions.
- Print your presentation.
- Deliver your presentation.

Lesson Introduction

Congratulations! You are ready to deliver your presentation. Or rather, you're almost ready to deliver it. You have a clear message that is well organized, and one that you have supported with images and numerical data. However, nothing kills credibility like glaring mistakes on your slides as you deliver your presentation. You will want to review and polish your work before stepping up to the podium. Additionally, there may be particular considerations you need to address for your specific situation. Does the audience require handouts? Will you need to archive or share your presentation after the event?

PowerPoint 2010 provides you with a variety of options for reviewing, revising, printing, and presenting your work. Becoming familiar with these functions will help you transform your presentation from a file on a computer to a real-life event that makes an impact on your audience.

TOPIC A

Review Your Presentation

It's been a while since you started adding text to your presentation. Before you get in front of a live audience, you want to make sure your text is perfect. After all, it's your credibility that is on the line. But mistakes aren't the only things that can be distracting to an audience. Have you used the same word too many times? Do you need to add some variety to your text?

PowerPoint 2010 offers you a number of tools that can help you deliver a clean, accurate presentation. Making a habit of checking your work before presenting can help you avoid some common presentation-delivery pitfalls.

AutoCorrect Feature Options

The AutoCorrect feature automatically corrects common spelling mistakes as you type. AutoCorrect will also correct common capitalization and text-formatting issues, and can insert mathematical symbols when you type the symbol names. You can customize the AutoCorrect feature by selecting the types of errors it will correct for you. You can access the **AutoCorrect** dialog box via the **Options** tab in **Backstage** view.

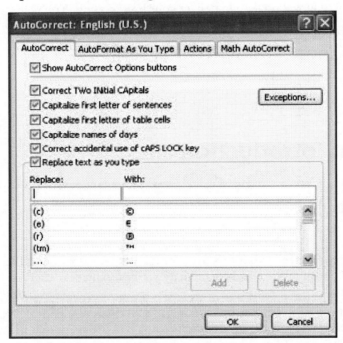

Figure 8-1: The AutoCorrect dialog box provides options for customizing the AutoCorrect feature.

AutoCorrect Dialog Box Tab	Provides Options For
AutoCorrect	Correcting spelling and capitalization errors, and correcting text typed with the **Caps Lock** key enabled.
AutoFormat As You Type	Formatting fractions and symbols, and for common text formatting like bulleted lists.
Actions	Creating additional actions for right-click menus when you type particular words.

AutoCorrect Dialog Box Tab	Provides Options For
Math AutoCorrect	Replacing typed text with mathematical symbols.

The Spell Checker Feature

The *spell checker feature* scans all of the text in your presentation looking for spelling errors. The spell checker feature compares the text on your slides and in the notes pane against a built-in list of words based on your language settings. Spelling errors will launch the **Spelling** dialog box, which gives you a set of options for how you would like PowerPoint to treat the misspelled word. You can access the spell checker in the **Proofing** group on the **Review** tab.

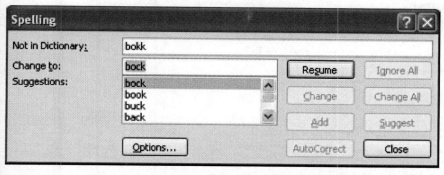

Figure 8-2: The Spelling dialog box lets you decide how to resolve spelling errors.

Spelling Dialog Box Element	Description
Not in Dictionary field	Displays the misspelled word.
Change to field	Displays the word that will replace the misspelled word.
Suggestions field	Displays a list of possible correct spellings for the misspelled word.
Ignore button	Leaves the current instance of the misspelled word as is.
Ignore All button	Leaves all instances of the misspelled word as they are.
Change button	Replaces the current instance of the misspelled word with the word in the **Change to** field.
Change All button	Replaces all instances of the misspelled word with the word in the **Change to** field.
Add button	Adds the misspelled word to the dictionary. Once this is done, the spell checker will no longer consider the word a misspelling.
Suggest button	Suggests a word from the **Suggestion** field to replace the misspelled word.
AutoCorrect button	Adds the misspelled word to the AutoCorrect list.

The Research Task Pane

The *Research task pane* provides you with options for performing research using a wide range of resources, both from your computer and online. You can use the Research task pane to look up word definitions, search for synonyms, or perform internet searches. You can access the **Research** task pane by selecting **Research** in the **Proofing** group on the **Review** tab.

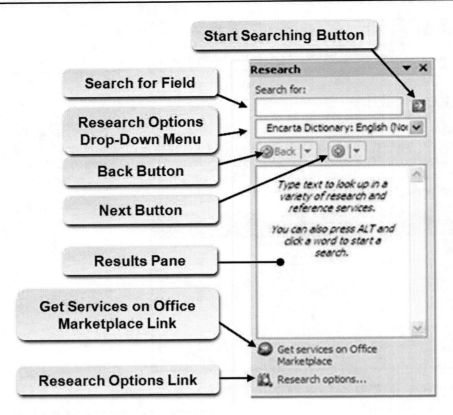

Figure 8–3: The Research task pane.

Research Task Pane Element	Function
Search for field	Displays the word or subject that you would like to research.
Start Searching button	Begins the desired search.
Research Options drop-down menu	Allows you to choose and displays the desired research resource for a particular search.
Back button	Navigates to the previous search result.
Next button	Navigates to the next search result. The **Next** button becomes active only once you have navigated backward through search results.
Results pane	Displays the research search results.
Get Services on Office Marketplace link	Links you to a list of third-party research services on Office.microsoft.com.
Research Options link	Launches the **Research Options** dialog box, which allows you to customize the resources available in the **Research Options** drop-down menu.

The Thesaurus

The *thesaurus* is a research tool that provides you with a list of synonyms and antonyms for a particular word. The thesaurus feature returns search results in the **Research** task pane. You can access the thesaurus in the **Proofing** group on the **Review** tab.

 Access the Checklist tile on your LogicalCHOICE course screen for reference information and job aids on How to Review Your Presentation

ACTIVITY 8–1
Reviewing Your Presentations

Data Files

Develetech Ind_charts linked.pptx

Scenario

You and the other members of the design teams have finished adding all of the content for the presentation, and all preliminary reviews are complete. You decide it would be a good idea to check the presentation for spelling errors before submitting the presentation for final approval.

---

1. Open the **Develetech Ind_charts linked.pptx** file from the C:\091031Data\Preparing to Deliver Your Presentation folder. Update the links when prompted.

2. Check the presentation for spelling errors.
   a) Select **Review→Proofing→Spelling**.
   b) When the **Spelling** dialog box is displayed, verify that "Gaming" is the appropriate word for the text, and then select **Change**.
   c) When the **Spelling** dialog box is displayed, verify that "Networking" is the appropriate word for the text, and then select **Change**.
   d) In the **Microsoft PowerPoint** dialog box, select **OK**.

3. Save the file as *My Develetech Ind_charts linked.pptx*

TOPIC B

Apply Transitions

You have corrected all of the spelling and grammatical errors in your presentation, and you have freshened up your text by replacing over-used words with synonyms. You could deliver your presentation as is and have a successful event. However, you want your presentation to really stand out. Repeatedly presenting one slide after another with no transition effects can get monotonous for the audience. You may want to add some flair to the transitions between your slides.

PowerPoint 2010 contains a host of on-board transition effects that can liven up your presentation. You can also apply slide transitions to emphasize slides that convey an important point.

Transitions

Transitions are visual effects that occur as you advance from one slide to the next in a presentation. PowerPoint 2010 includes a wide array of transition effects that you can apply to the slides in you presentation. You can modify the speed of transitions, change transition attributes such as direction or shape, and add sounds to transitions. Transitions can play automatically, respond to keystrokes or mouse clicks, or play after a specified period of time. You can access the **Transitions** gallery from the **Transition to This Slide** group on the **Transitions** tab.

	Note: Once you apply a transition to a slide, a star will appear along with the slide in the **Normal** and **Slide Sorter** views.

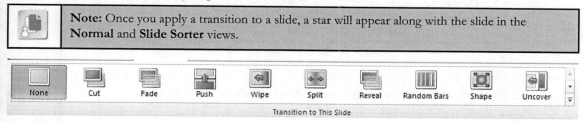
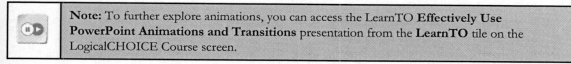

Figure 8-4: PowerPoint 2010 offers you a variety of slide transitions.

	Note: To further explore animations, you can access the LearnTO **Effectively Use PowerPoint Animations and Transitions** presentation from the **LearnTO** tile on the LogicalCHOICE Course screen.

	Access the Checklist tile on your LogicalCHOICE course screen for reference information and job aids on How to Work with Transitions

ACTIVITY 8-2
Applying Transitions

Before You Begin
The My Develetech Ind_charts linked.pptx file is open.

Scenario
You submitted the presentation to your supervisor for final approval. She approved the content and the overall look of the presentation, but she feels the still transitions between the slides are too dull for the subject matter. She has asked you to add transitions between the slides to add more energy to the presentation.

1. Add a transition between slides.
   a) Navigate to slide 2 in the left pane.
   b) Access the **Transitions** tab and, in the **Transition to this Slide** group, select the **More** button ⬇ to display the **Transitions** gallery.
   c) In the **Transitions** gallery, select **Switch** from the **Exciting** section.

2. Preview the transition by selecting the **Preview** button in the **Preview** group.

3. Modify the transition.
   a) In the **Transition to This Slide** group, select **Effect Options**.
   b) Select **Left** from the drop-down menu.
   c) In the **Timing** group, use **Duration** field's **spin buttons** to change the transition duration to 2 seconds.
   d) Preview the transition to verify the changes.

4. Apply the transition to all slides in the presentation.
   a) In the **Timing** group, Select **Apply To All**.
   b) Verify that the transition has been applied to all slides by navigating through the slides in the **left** pane and ensuring that a star is displayed next to the slides.
   c) Preview the transitions by navigating to various slides and selecting **Preview** in the **Preview** group.

5. Select **File→Save**.

TOPIC C

Print Your Presentation

Your presentation is now complete! At this point you are confident that you can stand in front of the audience and deliver an effective, engaging, high-impact presentation. However, you might want to reference your speaker notes to ensure you don't skip any important information during the presentation. Additionally, you may wish to print handouts to help the audience keep track of the presentation, or to take notes.

PowerPoint 2010 gives you several options for printing hard copies of your presentation depending on your particular need. In addition to giving you the security of having your content in hand during a presentation, access to hard copies can be a lifesaver in the event of a computer crash or other technical problem.

The Print Command

The *Print command* provides you with a variety of options for printing hard copies of your presentation, both for your benefit and the benefit of the audience. You can access the print command and options from the **Backstage** view by selecting the **File** tab on the ribbon. When you select the **Print** tab, the **Backstage** view displays two panes. The left pane displays the print settings and print options, whereas the right pane displays a preview of the currently selected print options. You can use the commands in the left pane to tailor the print options to suit your needs.

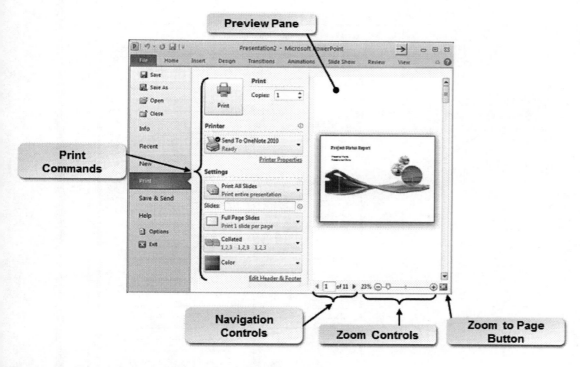

Figure 8–5: The Print command in the Backstage view.

Print Option	Allows You To
Print	Select the number of copies you wish to print, and print your presentation.

Print Option	Allows You To
Printer drop-down menu	Select your printing destination.
Print All Slides drop-down menu	Select between printing all slides or printing only certain slides.
Slides field	Determine which slides to print if you are not printing the entire presentation.
Full Page Slides drop-down menu	Select from among printing full page slides, notes, outlines, or handouts. You can also set other printing options such as scaling the printing to fit the paper.
Print One Side drop-down menu	Switch between printing on one side of the paper or both sides.
Collated drop-down menu	Choose between collating or not collating your printouts.
Grayscale drop-down menu	Select full-color printing, grayscale printing, or black and white printing.

Handouts

Handouts are printed materials that the audience can use to follow along with a presentation and take notes. In addition to printing handouts by using the **Print** command, you can use PowerPoint to create a Microsoft Word document version of your handouts. Typically, the handouts will display page numbers and the presentation date for the audience to reference.

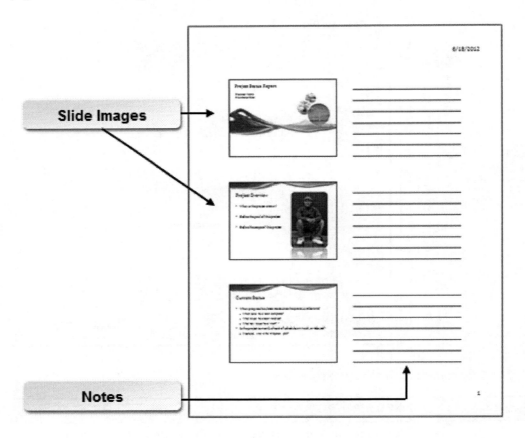

Figure 8–6: A PowerPoint handout with three slides displayed per page.

Outlines

Outlines are printed materials that display all of the text, but none of the graphics, from the slides in a presentation. The text is displayed along with the slide numbers to help people follow along with the presentation.

Figure 8-7: A presentation outline.

Notes Pages

Notes pages are printed materials that show the speaker notes, slide numbers, and the images from slides in a presentation. This printout is ideal for delivering your presentation.

Figure 8-8: A notes page from a PowerPoint presentation.

Full Page Slides

Full page slides are printed materials that display the slides in a presentation only. Full page slides do not include speaker notes or space for the audience to take notes. On screen text, however, is displayed as it is shown on the slides.

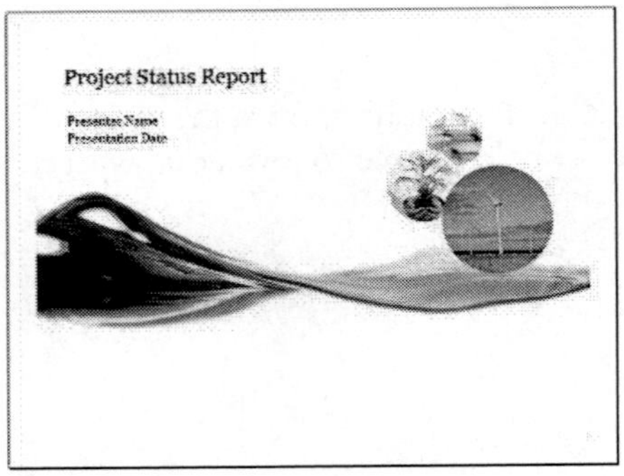

Figure 8-9: A full page slide from a PowerPoint presentation.

Access the Checklist tile on your LogicalCHOICE course screen for reference information and job aids on How to Print Your Presentation

ACTIVITY 8–3
Setting Your Print Options

Before You Begin
The My Develetech Ind_charts linked.pptx file is open.

Scenario
The presentation is now complete! One of your colleagues will be delivering the first presentation. She has asked you to print one set of notes for her to use during the presentation. She will need notes for slides 1 through 13 only. You realize you will need to adjust the print options before printing.

---

1. Select the **File** tab to access the **Backstage** view.

2. Set your print options.
   a) Select the **Print** tab.
   b) In the **Settings** section, into the **Slides** field of the left pane, type *1-13*.
   c) Verify that the drop-down menu above the **Slides** field is displayed as **Custom Range**.
   d) Select the **Full Page Slides** drop-down menu below the **Slides** field, and then select **Notes Pages** from the **Print Layout** section of the drop-down menu.

3. Use the **Next Page** and **Previous Page** buttons at the bottom of the right pane to preview your notes pages.

4. Select **Save** from the left pane.

TOPIC D

Deliver Your Presentation

The day is here, you are just about to deliver your presentation. You have your printed notes to reference during the event, and you have printed and passed out the audience handouts. All that is left is to deliver your presentation while displaying the slides to the audience. So, how do you do that, exactly? And, what if you want to share your ideas with people who aren't in the room?

PowerPoint 2010 contains robust functionality for customizing your slide shows and for saving your presentations in various formats. These options give you complete control over your live presentation and allow you to share your content with everyone who needs to hear the message.

Presentation Options

Typically, during a slide show the computer from which you deliver your presentation will be connected to a projector or you will be sharing your desktop in a web-conferencing application. This allows the audience members to view your slides as your present. There are four basic options for delivering your presentations in PowerPoint 2010: from the beginning, from the current slide, as a web broadcast, or as a custom slide show. You can access these options on the **Slide Show** tab in the **Start Slide Show** group.

Figure 8–10: The Slide Show tab.

Slide Show Option	Displays Your Slide Show
From Beginning	From the first slide in sequential order.
From Current Slide	From the currently selected slide in sequential order.
Broadcast Slide Show	As a web-based broadcast that can be viewed by anyone with an Internet connection. You will need a Windows Live ID to broadcast a slide show.
Custom Slide Show	In a pre-determined fashion. Custom slide shows must be set up ahead of time, and will display only the selected slides.

 Access the Checklist tile on your LogicalCHOICE course screen for reference information and job aids on **How to Present a Slide Show**

ACTIVITY 8–4
Presenting a Slide Show

Before You Begin
The My Develetech Ind_charts linked.pptx file is open.

Scenario
Your colleague has asked you to run the slide show as she delivers the presentation.

1. Select **Slide Show→Start Slide Show→From Beginning**.

2. Navigate through the slides and animations by clicking the screen.

3. Press the **Esc** key to exit the slide show.

PowerPoint Presentation File Formats

Delivering your presentation live in front of an audience isn't the only way in which you can share it. PowerPoint 2010 provides you with multiple file format options for saving your presentation. The various file formats provide you with a number of different outputs, such as outlines or images, that are well suited for various uses. You can save your presentations in various file formats from the **Backstage** view. The table following the figure lists some of the more commonly used file-saving options.

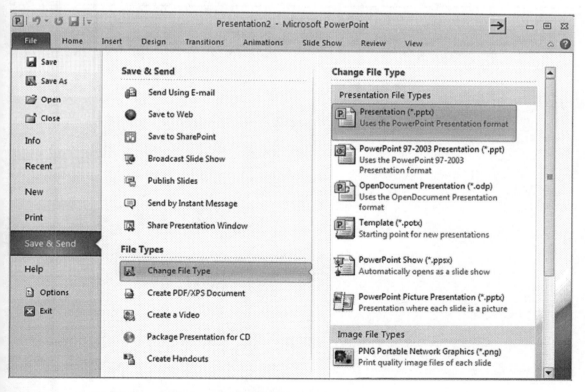

Figure 8–11: File saving options in the Backstage view.

File Saving Option (File Extension)	Description
PowerPoint Picture Presentation (.pptx)	A PowerPoint presentation for which all slides have been converted to a picture. This reduces file size, making picture presentations ideal for storing and sharing via email. However, some information is lost.
Portable Document Format (.pdf)/XML Paper Specification (.xps)	Saving the presentation as an .xps or a .pdf file creates a digital document that preserves formatting and makes the presentation easy to view on nearly all computers. This is ideal for sharing your presentation via email, or archiving it to a directory.
Outline (.rtf)	Saves the on-screen text from your presentation as an outline. This creates a much smaller file that is ideal for reviewing the presentation or sharing only the key points.
Open Document Presentation (.odp)	Allows you to open the presentation in presentation applications other than PowerPoint. You can also open .odp files in PowerPoint 2010. Some information may be lost when saving to or opening .odp files.
PowerPoint Show (.ppsx)	A PowerPoint presentation that, by default, opens in the Slide Show view, not the **Normal** view. This is ideal for sharing the presentation with people who will also deliver it, but will not need to change the content.
Save a Slide or an Object as a Picture File (.jpg, .png)	Saves a single slide or an object as an image file.

 Access the Checklist tile on your LogicalCHOICE course screen for reference information and job aids on How to Save Your Presentation in Various File Formats

ACTIVITY 8–5
Saving a Presentation as a PDF

Before You Begin
The My Develetech Ind_charts linked.pptx file is open.

Scenario
Your colleague has asked you to email a PDF of the presentation to all of the attendees. You will first need to save the presentation as a PDF file.

1. Access the **Backstage** view by selecting the **File** tab.

2. Select the **Save As** command, and then navigate to the desktop in the **Save As** dialog box.

3. In the **File name** field, enter *My Develetech Ind*

4. Select **PDF** from the **Save as type** drop-down menu.

5. Select **Save**.

6. Close the My Develetech Ind.pdf file, and then close PowerPoint 2010.

Summary

You have successfully delivered your PowerPoint presentation. Using the various features in PowerPoint 2010 for reviewing, polishing, delivering, and sharing your presentations will give you the confidence you need to present important information whenever the need may arise. And, you now have the flexibility of knowing you can present to an audience under a variety of circumstances and using differing technology.

What do you think is the most important aspect of preparing for a presentation?

Can you see a downside to using transitions in your presentations?

 Note: Check your LogicalCHOICE Course screen for opportunities to interact with your classmates, peers, and the larger LogicalCHOICE online community about the topics covered in this course or other topics you are interested in. From the Course screen you can also access available resources for a more continuous learning experience.

Course Follow-Up

You have completed the Microsoft® Office PowerPoint® 2010: Part 1 course! You have successfully created and developed engaging multimedia presentations that use text, graphics, and animations to convey key points of your message.

The ability to communicate important information in a variety of situations will continue to be a critical skill in an increasingly connected world. In fact, it is likely to grow in importance as methods of communication become faster and more mobile. But, with an increase in the number of messages people encounter daily comes a massive amount clutter that can be difficult to penetrate. The effective use of engaging, dynamic, multimedia presentations is one way you can cut through the noise, and make your point. Develop PowerPoint presentations that are clear and succinct, use graphical content to support your content, and contain effects and animations that will grab the audience's attention.

What's Next?

Microsoft® Office PowerPoint® 2010: Part 2 is the next course in this series. In that course, you will customize the PowerPoint environment to streamline your workflow, enhance your presentation by using more advanced graphics and animations features, collaborate on your presentation with colleagues, and utilize advanced slide show and sharing features. You are also encouraged to explore PowerPoint further by actively participating in any of the social media forums set up by your instructor or training administrator through the **Social Media** tile on the LogicalCHOICE Course screen.

A | Microsoft Office PowerPoint 2010 Exam 77-883

Selected Logical Operations courseware addresses Microsoft Office Specialist (MOS) certification skills for Microsoft Office 2010. The following table indicates where PowerPoint 2010 skills that are tested on Exam 77-883 are covered in the Logical Operations Microsoft Office PowerPoint 2010 series of courses.

Objective Domain	Covered In
1. Managing the PowerPoint Environment	
1.1 Adjust views	
1.1.1 Adjust views using the ribbon	Part 1, Topic 2-B
1.1.2 Adjust views by status bar commands	Part 1, Topics 1-A, 2-B
1.2 Manipulate the PowerPoint window	
1.2.1 Work with multiple presentation windows simultaneously	Part 2
1.3 Configure the Quick Access toolbar	
1.3.1 Show the QAT below the ribbon	Part 2
1.4 Configure the PPT file options	
1.4.1 Use PPT proofing	Part 1, Topic 8-A
1.4.2 Use PPT save options	Part 1, Topic 8-D
2. Creating a Slide Presentation	
2.1 Construct and edit photo albums	
2.1.1 Add captions to picture	Part 1, Topic 4-A
2.1.2 Insert text	Part 1, Topic 4-A
2.1.3 Insert images in black and white	Part 1, Topic 4-A
2.1.4 Reorder pictures in an album	Part 1, Topic 4-A
2.1.5 Adjust image	Part 1, Topic 4-A
2.1.5.1 Rotation	Part 1, Topic 4-A
2.1.5.2 Brightness	Part 1, Topic 4-A
2.1.5.3 Contrast	Part 1, Topic 4-A

Objective Domain	Covered In
2.2 Apply slide size and orientation settings	
2.2.1 Set up a custom size	Part 1, Topic 2-D
2.2.2 Change the orientation	Part 1, Topic 2-D
2.3 Add and remove slides	
2.3.1 Insert an outline	Part 1, Topic 2-A
2.3.2 Reuse slides from a saved presentation	Part 1, Topic 2-D
2.3.3 Reuse slides from a slides library	Part 2,
2.3.4 Duplicate selected slides	Part 1, Topic 2-D
2.3.5 Duplicate multiple slides simultaneously	Part 1, Topic 2-D
2.3.6 Include noncontiguous slides in a presentation	Part 1, Topic 2-D
2.4 Format slides	
2.4.1 Format sections	Part 2
2.4.2 Modify themes	Part 1, Topic 2-D
2.4.3 Switch to a different slide layout	Part 1, Topic 2-D
2.4.4 Apply formatting to a slide	
2.4.4.1 Fill color	Part 1, Topic 2-D
2.4.4.2 Gradient	Part 1, Topic 2-D
2.4.4.3 Picture	Part 1, Topic 2-D
2.4.4.4 Texture	Part 1, Topic 2-D
2.4.4.5 Pattern	Part 1, Topic 2-D
2.4.5 Set up slide footers	Part 2
2.5 Enter and format text	
2.5.1 use text effects	Part 1, Topic 3-A
2.5.2 Change text format	
2.5.2.1 Indentation	Part 1, Topic 3-B
2.5.2.2 Alignment	Part 1, Topic 3-B
2.5.2.3 Line spacing	Part 1, Topic 3-B
2.5.2.4 Direction	Part 1, Topic 3-B
2.5.3 Change the formatting of bulleted and numbered lists	Part 1, Topic 3-B
2.5.4 Enter text in a placeholder text box	Part 1, Topics 1-B, 2-C
2.5.5 Convert text to SmartArt	Part 2
2.5.6 Copy and paste text	Part 1, Topic 2-C
2.5.7 Use paste special	Part 1, Topic 2-C
2.5.8 Use format painter	Part 1, Topic 3-A
2.6 Format text boxes	
2.6.1 Apply formatting to a text box	

Objective Domain	Covered In
2.6.1.1 Fill color	Part 1, Topic 3-C
2.6.1.2 Gradient	Part 1, Topic 3-C
2.6.1.3 Picture	Part 1, Topic 3-C
2.6.1.4 Texture	Part 1, Topic 3-C
2.6.1.5 Pattern	Part 1, Topic 3-C
2.6.2 Change the outline of a text box	
2.6.2.1 Color	Part 1, Topic 3-C
2.6.2.2 Weight	Part 1, Topic 3-C
2.6.2.3 Style	Part 1, Topic 3-C
2.6.3 Change the shape of a text box	Part 1, Topic 4-B
2.6.4 Apply effects	Part 1, Topic 3-C
2.6.5 Set the alignment	Part 1, Topic 3-B
2.6.6 Create columns in a text box	Part 1, Topic 3-B
2.6.7 Set internal margins	Part 1, Topic 3-C
2.6.8 Set the current text box formatting as the default for new text boxes	Part 1, Topic 3-C
2.6.9 Adjust text in a text box	
2.6.9.1 Wrap	Part 1, Topics 4-A, 4-B
2.6.9.2 Size	Part 1, Topic 3-A
2.6.9.3 Position	Part 1, Topic 3-B
2.6.10 Use auto-fit	Part 1, Topic 3-B
3. Working with Graphical and Multimedia Elements	
3.1 Manipulate graphical elements	
3.1.1 Arrange graphical elements	Part 1, Topic 5-D
3.1.2 Position graphical elements	Part 1, Topic 5-D
3.1.3 Resize graphical elements	Part 1, Topics 2-C, 5-A
3.1.4 Apply effects to graphical elements	Part 1, Topic 5-B
3.1.5 Apply styles to graphical elements	Part 1, Topic 5-B
3.1.6 Apply borders to graphical elements	Part 1, Topic 5-B
3.1.7 Apply hyperlinks to graphical elements	Part 2
3.2 Manipulate images	
3.2.1 Apply color adjustments	Part 1, Topic 5-A
3.2.2 Apply image corrections	
3.2.2.1 Sharpen	Part 1, Topic 5-A
3.2.2.2 Soften	Part 1, Topic 5-A
3.2.2.3 Brightness	Part 1, Topic 5-A
3.2.2.4 Contrast	Part 1, Topic 5-A

Objective Domain	Covered In
3.2.3 Add artistic effects to an image	Part 1, Topics 5-A, 5-B
3.2.4 Remove a background	Part 1, Topic 5-A
3.2.5 Crop a picture	Part 1, Topic 5-A
3.2.6 Compress selected pictures/all pictures	Part 1, Topic 5-A
3.2.7 Change a picture	Part 1, Topic 5-A
3.2.8 Reset a picture	Part 1, Topic 5-A
3.3 Modify WordArt and shapes	
3.3.1 Set the formatting of the current shape as the default for future shapes	Part 1, Topic 4-B
3.3.2 Change the fill color or texture	Part 1, Topic 4-B
3.3.3 Change the WordArt	Part 1, Topic 3-A
3.3.4 Convert WordArt to SmartArt	Part 2
3.4 Manipulate SmartArt	
3.4.1 Add and remove shapes	Part 1, Topic 4-B
3.4.2 Change SmartArt styles	Part 2
3.4.3 Change the SmartArt layout	Part 2
3.4.4 Reorder shapes	Part 2
3.4.5 Convert a SmartArt graphic to text	Part 2
3.4.6 Convert SmartArt to shapes	Part 2
3.4.7 Make shapes larger or smaller	Part 2
3.4.8 Promote bullet levels	Part 2
3.4.9 Demote bullet levels	Part 2
3.5 Edit video and audio content	
3.5.1 Apply a style to video or audio content	Part 2
3.5.2 Adjust video or audio content	Part 2
3.5.3 Arrange video or audio content	Part 2
3.5.4 Size video or audio content	Part 2
3.5.5 Adjust playback options	Part 2
4. Creating Charts and Tables	
4.1 Construct and modify tables	
4.1.1 Draw a table	Part 1, Topic 6-A
4.1.2 Insert a Microsoft Excel spreadsheet	Part 1, Topic 6-C
4.1.3 Set table and style options	Part 1, Topic 6-B
4.1.4 Add shading	Part 1, Topics 6-B, 6-C
4.1.5 Add borders	Part 1, Topic 6-B
4.1.6 Add effects	Part 1, Topic 6-B
4.1.7 Columns and rows	

Objective Domain	Covered In
4.1.7.1 Change the alignment	Part 1, Topic 6-B
4.1.7.2 Resize	Part 1, Topic 6-B
4.1.7.3 Merge	Part 1, Topic 6-B
4.1.7.4 Split	Part 1, Topic 6-B
4.1.7.5 Distribute	Part 1, Topic 6-B
4.1.7.6 Arrange	Part 1, Topic 6-B
4.2 Insert and modify charts	
4.2.1 Select a chart type	Part 1, Topic 7-A
4.2.2 Enter chart data	Part 1, Topic 7-A
4.2.3 Change the chart type	Part 1, Topic 7-B
4.2.4 Change the chart layout	Part 1, Topic 7-B
4.2.5 Switch row and column	Part 1, Topic 7-B
4.2.6 Select data	Part 1, Topic 7-A
4.2.7 Edit data	Part 1, Topic 7-A
4.3 Apply chart elements	
4.3.1 Use chart labels	Part 1, Topic 7-B
4.3.2 Use axes	Part 1, Topic 7-B
4.3.3 Use gridlines	Part 1, Topic 7-B
4.3.4 Use backgrounds	Part 1, Topic 7-B
4.4 Manipulate chart layouts	
4.4.1 Select chart elements	Part 1, Topic 7-B
4.4.2 Format selections	Part 1, Topic 7-B
4.5 Manipulate chart elements	
4.5.1 Arrange chart elements	Part 1, Topic 7-B
4.5.2 Specify a precise position	Part 1, Topic 7-B
4.5.3 Apply effects	Part 1, Topic 7-B
4.5.4 Resize chart elements	Part 1, Topic 7-B
4.5.5 Apply quick styles	Part 1, Topic 7-B
4.5.6 Apply a border	Part 1, Topic 7-B
4.5.7 Add hyperlinks	Part 2
5. Applying Transitions and Animations	
5.1 Apply built-in and custom animations	
5.1.1 Use more entrance	Part 2
5.1.2 Use more emphasis	Part 2
5.1.3 Use more exit effects	Part 2
5.1.4 Use more motion paths	Part 2

Objective Domain	Covered In
5.2 Apply effect and path options	
5.2.1 Set timing	Part 2
5.2.2 Set start options	Part 2
5.3 Manipulate animations	
5.3.1 Change the direction of animations	Part 1, Topic 5-E
5.3.2 Attach a sound to an animation	Part 2
5.3.3 Use Animation Painter	Part 1, Topic 5-E
5.3.4 Reorder animation	Part 2
5.3.5 Selecting text options	Part 2
5.4 Apply and modify transitions between slides	
5.4.1 Modify a transition effect	Part 1, Topic 8-B
5.4.2 Add a sound to a transition	Part 1, Topic 8-B
5.4.3 Modify transition duration	Part 1, Topic 8-B
5.4.4 Set up manual or automatically timed advance options	Part 2
6. Collaborating on Presentations	
6.1 Manage comments in presentations	
6.1.1 Insert and edit comments	Part 2
6.1.2 Show or hide markup	Part 2
6.1.3 Move to the previous or next comment	Part 2
6.1.4 Delete comments	Part 2
6.2 Apply proofing tools	
6.2.1 Use spelling and thesaurus features	Part 1, Topic 8-A
6.2.2 Compare and combine presentations	Part 2
7. Preparing Presentations for Delivery	
7.1 Save presentations	Part 1, Topic 8-D
7.1.1 Save the presentation as a picture	Part 1, Topic 8-D
7.1.2 Save the presentation as a PDF	Part 1, Topic 8-D
7.1.3 Save the presentation as an XPS	Part 1, Topic 8-D
7.1.4 Save the presentation as an outline	Part 1, Topic 8-D
7.1.5 Save the presentation an open document	Part 1, Topic 8-D
7.1.6 Save the presentation as a show (.ppsx)	Part 1, Topic 8-D
7.1.7 Save a slide or object as a picture file	Part 1, Topic 8-D
7.2 Share presentations	
7.2.1 Share a presentation for CD delivery	Part 2
7.2.2 Create video	Part 2
7.2.3 Create handouts	Part 1, Topic 8-D

Objective Domain	Covered In
7.2.4 Compress media	Part 2
7.3 Print presentations	
7.3.1 Adjust print settings	Part 1, Topics 8-C, 8-D
7.4 Protect presentations	
7.4.1 Set a password	Part 2
7.4.2 Change a password	Part 2
7.4.3 Mark a presentation as final	Part 2
8. Delivering Presentations	
8.1 Apply presentation tools	
8.1.1 Add pen and highlighter annotations	Part 2
8.1.2 Change the ink color	Part 2
8.1.3 Erase an annotation	Part 2
8.1.4 Discard annotations upon closing	Part 2
8.1.5 Retain annotations upon closing	Part 2
8.2 Set up slide shows	
8.2.1 Set up a slide show	Part 2
8.2.2 Play narrations	Part 2
8.2.3 Set up presenter view	Part 2
8.2.4 Use timings	Part 1, Topic 8-D
8.2.5 Show media controls	Part 2
8.2.6 Broadcast presentations	Part 2
8.2.7 Create a custom slide show	Part 2
8.3 Set presentation timing	
8.3.1 Rehearse timings	Part 2
8.3.2 Keep timings	Part 2
8.3.3 Adjust a slide's timing	Part 1, Topic 8-D
8.4 Record presentations	
8.4.1 Start recording from the beginning of slide show	Part 2
8.4.2 Start recording from the current slide of the slide show	Part 2

Microsoft PowerPoint 2010 Common Keyboard Shortcuts

The following table lists common keyboard shortcuts you can use in PowerPoint 2010.

Function	Shortcut
Change the font of selected text	Ctrl + Shift + F
Change the font size of selected text	Ctrl + Shift + P
Open the **Find** dialog box	Ctrl + F
Copy the selected text	Ctrl + C
Paste copied content	Ctrl + V
Select all	Ctrl + A
Undo the last action	Ctrl + Z
Apply or remove bold formatting	Ctrl + B
Apply or remove italic formatting	Ctrl + I
Apply or remove underline formatting	Ctrl + U
Insert a hyperlink	Ctrl + K
Center a paragraph	Ctrl + E
Justify a paragraph	Ctrl + J
Left align a paragraph	Ctrl + L
Right align a paragraph	Ctrl + R
Start a presentation from the beginning	F5
Advance to the next slide	N or Enter
Return to the previous slide	P or Backspace
Go to slide *number*	*number* + Enter
End a presentation	Esc
View the **All Slides** dialog box	Ctrl + S
Increase sound volume	Alt + Up
Decrease sound volume	Alt + Down

Lesson Labs

Lesson labs are provided for certain lessons as additional learning resources for this course. Lesson labs are developed for selected lessons within a course in cases when they seem most instructionally useful as well as technically feasible. In general, labs are supplemental, optional unguided practice and may or may not be performed as part of the classroom activities. Your instructor will consider setup requirements, classroom timing, and instructional needs to determine which labs are appropriate for you to perform, and at what point during the class. If you do not perform the labs in class, your instructor can tell you if you can perform them independently as self-study, and if there are any special setup requirements.

Lesson Lab 2-1
Creating a Presentation

Activity Time: 10 minutes

Data File
Design Team Review Process.docx

Before You Begin
Open the Design Team Review Process.docx file from the C:\091031Data
\Developing a PowerPoint Presentation folder.

Scenario
At an upcoming development team meeting, your team will be compiling ideas for a
new design review process. You have volunteered to create a PowerPoint presentation
that will be used to present the ideas to your department's director. Your team will
populate the presentation with the team's best ideas. For easy comparison, you decide
to include the old process highlights from an existing document.

1. Launch PowerPoint 2010.

2. Enter the title *Proposed Review Processes* and the subtitle *A New Way Forward*.

3. Apply the **Urban** theme to the presentation.

4. Insert two Section Header slides as slides 2 and 3.

5. Enter the title *Old Process* and the subtitle *Highlights* on slide 2.

6. Enter the title *Proposed Process* and the subtitle *Highlights* on slide 3.

7. Insert two blank slides as slides 4 and 5.

8. Copy and paste the "High Level Process" text and the bulleted list from the Word
   document to slide 4, keeping the source formatting.

9. Close the Word document.

10. Move slide 4 so that it follows slide 2.

11. Apply a pattern fill to the background of all slides.

12. Save the file to the C:\091031Data\Developing a PowerPoint Presentation folder as *My
    Proposal.pptx*.

13. Close the file.

Lesson Lab 3-1
Editing Text

Activity Time: 10 minutes

Data File

Media 201.pptx

Before You Begin

Open the Media 201.pptx file from the C:\091031Data\Performing Advanced Text Editing folder.

Scenario

You are a communications professor at a local community college. You are putting together an orientation presentation for the students on the first day of class. So far, you have only included default text on the slides in your presentation. You know this will not hold the students' interest, so you decide to apply text formatting to make the presentation look better.

1. Apply a WordArt style to the title text on slide 1.

2. Change the font of the subtitle text on slide 1 to Arial Black, change the font color to dark blue, and change the font size to 28.

3. Apply a different WordArt style from the one you used on slide 1 to the title text on slide 2.

4. Use the Format Painter to apply the formatting from the title text on slide 2 to the title text on slides 3 through 6.

5. Change the numbered list on slide 2 to a bulleted list.

6. Change the existing text on slide 5 into a bulleted list with "Groups will:" as a header, removing "Groups will" from each of the bullets in the list.

7. Add a border and a gradient fill to the text box on slide 2.

8. Set the text box formatting from the text box on slide 2 as the default text box formatting.

9. Copy and paste the text box formatting from slide 2 to the text boxes on the remaining slides.

10. Add a text box to slide 6, and then type *?* into the text box.

11. Center the "?" in the text box on slide 6 both horizontally and vertically.

12. Increase the font size of the "?" to 100, and then move the text box so that it is centered below the title text.

13. Save the file as *My Media 201.pptx*, and then close the file.

Lesson Lab 4–1
Adding Clip Art and Images

Activity Time: 10 minutes

Data Files

Company Awards.pptx

Group.jpg

Before You Begin

Open the Company Awards.pptx file from the C:\091031Data\Adding Graphical Elements to Your Presentation folder.

Scenario

Your boss is delivering an awards presentation highlighting the accomplishments of the top performing departments within the company. Although all of the text is in place, your boss feels that an image representative of each of the departments would add to the presentation. She has asked you to add appropriate images to the slides for the winning departments.

---

1. Add the Group.jpg image from the C:\091031Data\Adding Graphical Elements to Your Presentation folder to slide 4.

2. Drag the image Group.jpg to the lower left corner of the slide.

3. Add a clip art photograph or an illustration of money to slide 5.

4. Drag the clip art to the lower left corner of the slide.

5. Draw a **Cloud** callout shape onto the lower left corner of slide 6.

6. Apply a shape style to the shape.

7. Save the file to the C:\091031Data\Adding Graphical Elements to Your Presentation folder as *My Company Awards.pptx*.

8. Close the file.

Lesson Lab 5-1
Working with Objects

Activity Time: 10 minutes

Data File
Winter Wonder.pptx

Before You Begin
Open the Winter Wonder.pptx file from the C:\091031Data\Modifying Objects in Your Presentation folder.

Scenario
You and your business partner own a ski and snowboarding shop. You are pitching your advertising ideas to a marketing agency that you view as a potential vendor. The goal of the marketing campaign is to get customers thinking about winter in terms of fun, not misery. You like the images you have selected for the presentation you will deliver, but you feel some of them could be a bit livelier. You decide to modify some of the images to help express your vision to the marketing agency's creative director.

1. Remove the background of the image of the skier on the right side of slide 2.

2. Place the image of the skier on slide 2 in front of the winter image so that it is centered.

3. Group the two images on slide 2 together, and then center the group horizontally on the slide.

4. Select only the image of the skier on slide 2, and then apply the **Set Transparent Color** feature to the center part of the image.

5. Apply the **Photocopy** artistic effect to the image of the skier on slide 3.

6. Scale the image of the cabin on slide 4 so that it is the same height as the image of the snowboarder.

7. Align the image of the cabin on slide 4 vertically with the image of the snowboarder, and then center it horizontally below the left text box.

8. Apply an animation effect to the image on slide 5 so that it flies in from the top-right corner of the slide.

9. Increase the speed of the animation effect.

10. Preview the animation effect.

11. Save the file to the C:\091031Data\Modifying Objects in Your Presentation folder as *My Winter Wonder.pptx*.

Lesson Lab 7-1
Working with Tables and Charts

Activity Time: 15 minutes

Data Files

Sales Meeting.pptx

Sales Overview.xlsx

Before You Begin

Open the Sales Meeting.pptx file from the C:\091031Data\Adding Charts to Your Presentation folder.

Scenario

You are concerned about the recent decrease in sales for your company compared to last fiscal year. You have called an emergency meeting with department heads to discuss the matter. You decide that presenting a chart that visually displays the sales drop will grab people's attention at the meeting. You have the sales figures in a Microsoft® Excel® worksheet, so you decide to add the worksheet to your presentation and to use the data from the worksheet to create the chart.

---

1. Enter *Sales Drop* in the title text placeholder on slide 4.

2. Create a table with five columns and three rows on slide 4.

3. Open the Sales Overview.xlsx file from the C:\091031Data\Adding Charts to Your Presentation folder, and then copy the information from the populated cells to the clipboard.

4. Paste the data from the Excel worksheet into the cells of the table on slide 4, and then close the Sales Overview.xlsx file.

5. Apply a table style to the table so that it fits well with the presentation.

6. Center the text in the table cells vertically and horizontally.

7. Increase the font size of the table text to 20.

8. Position the table so that it is aligned appropriately below the title text.

9. Create a **Clustered Bar in 3-D** chart on slide 5.

10. Modify the chart data worksheet so that it contains two categories and four series, and then delete all data outside of the range.

11. Copy and paste the data from the table on slide 4 into the chart data worksheet. Use the destination formatting.

12. Switch the X and the Y axes for the chart, and then close the chart data worksheet.

13. Change the chart type to **3-D Line**.

14. Add a title to the chart.

15. Apply formatting to the **Back Wall**, the **Side Wall**, and the **Floor**.

16. Increase the chart's height to 5.0" by scaling it up.

17. Center the chart on the slide.

18. Save the file to the C:\091031Data\Adding Charts to Your Presentation folder as *My Sales Meeting.pptx*.

19. Close the file.

Lesson Lab 8–1
Preparing for and Delivering a Presentation

Activity Time: 10 minutes

Data File

Winter Wonder Final.pptx

Before You Begin

Open the Winter Wonder Final.pptx file from the C:\091031Data\Preparing to Deliver Your Presentation folder.

Scenario

You are ready to deliver your marketing campaign presentation to a potential vendor for your ski and snowboard shop. You decide it would be a good idea to check for errors and to print your notes before the meeting. You also want to liven up the presentation by adding slide transitions.

1. Run the spell checker feature and correct the spelling errors in the presentation.

2. Use the thesaurus to select an alternate word for "Imagine" in the text above the image of the skier on slide 3.

3. Apply the **Shred** transition, with a duration of 1.5 seconds, to all slides in the presentation.

4. Use the **Print** command to review your slide notes.

5. Run a slide show to review the presentation.

6. Save the file to the C:\091031Data\Preparing to Deliver Your Presentation folder as *My Winter Wonder Final.pptx*.

7. Close PowerPoint 2010.

Glossary

Animation Painter
A PowerPoint feature that allows users to reapply animation effects to multiple objects.

AutoCorrect feature
A PowerPoint feature that automatically corrects common spelling and capitalization errors.

AutoFit feature
A PowerPoint feature that allows users to automatically fit text within text boxes and shapes regardless of the amount of text entered.

background styles
The colors and textures of slide backgrounds. These can be determined by applying themes to slides or through customization.

Backstage View
A PowerPoint user interface component that appears when users select the **File** tab. The **Backstage** view contains vertically aligned tabs that provide users with groups of related commands associated with managing files and configuring PowerPoint settings.

cells
Containers for numerical data and other content that make up a table.

character formats
Particular attributes that users can apply to the text in a presentation.

chart layouts
Pre-formatted or customizable options that determine which chart elements, such as labels, titles, and legends, will appear, and where they appear, on a chart.

chart styles
Quick styles that users can apply to charts.

charts
Graphical representations of numerical or mathematical data.

Clip Art
Digital graphical content that users can add to presentations.

clipboard
A task pane that allows users to paste copied text and graphical elements within Microsoft Office applications.

contextual tabs
Highly specialized tabs that appear on the ribbon when certain objects are selected. These contain specific commands and menus related to items such as tables, charts, and pictures.

cropping
Removing particular regions of an image to display only the desired image elements.

dialog box launchers
Small buttons with downward-facing arrows on the bottom-right corner of some ribbon functional groups. These buttons open dialog boxes that contain additional

commands specific to the functional groups.

embedding
The process of placing a copy of an object from a source file into a presentation. Changes in the source file are not reflected in the presentation.

Format Painter
A PowerPoint feature that allows users to copy object or text formatting, and then apply the formatting to other objects or text.

full page slides
Printed materials that display only the slides in a presentation.

galleries
Rectangular menus that display a variety of related visual options for objects in a presentation.

gridlines
Multiple horizontal and vertical dotted lines that form a grid, which allows users to accurately position objects on a slide.

Grouping feature
PowerPoint feature that allows users to link multiple objects together, effectively making them a single object.

guides
Lines that allow users to accurately position objects on a slide. By default, these lines divide slides into four equal sections and intersect at the exact center of the slides.

handouts
Printed materials that the audience can use to follow along with a presentation and take notes.

image compression
The process of reducing the file size of an image.

linking
The process of importing an object into a presentation in which the data is stored in the source file. When the source file is changed, the changes are reflected in the imported object.

Live Preview feature
PowerPoint feature that displays a temporary preview of formatting changes. This feature allows users to view various formatting options before they are selected.

Mini toolbar
A floating toolbar that appears next to selected objects on slides, and provides users with access to some of the most commonly used commands without having to navigate the ribbon.

notes pages
Printed materials that display the speaker notes, slide numbers, and the images from the slides in a presentation.

Notes Pane
A PowerPoint user interface component that allows users to enter notes that can be referenced during the delivery of a presentation.

object order
A function of PowerPoint that defines how objects that overlap on slides appear in relation to each other. The state of being located in front of or behind other objects.

orientation
The angle at which an object displays on a slide.

Outline tab
A PowerPoint user interface component that appears a view of the text from slides in a presentation in the left pane.

outlines
Printed materials that display all of the text, but none of the graphics, from the slides in a presentation.

Paste Preview
A PowerPoint feature that displays a temporary preview of a paste commands.

This feature allows users to view various pasting options before they are selected.

Paste Special command
A PowerPoint feature that allows users to paste objects to a new location as a specific type of file.

Photo Album feature
A PowerPoint feature that allows users to insert and display photographs in a custom presentation.

Print command
Provides users with a variety of options for printing hard copies of presentation.

Quick Access Toolbar
A PowerPoint user interface component that provides users with easy access to commonly used commands.

Quick Styles
Themes that can be quickly applied to a particular object by selecting a single command button.

Remove Background Tool
A PowerPoint feature that allows users to remove the background from images, leaving only the desired subject elements in the image.

Replace Fonts option
A PowerPoint feature that allows users to replace all text of a particular font type to another font type throughout a presentation.

Research task pane
A PowerPoint component that provides users with options for performing research by using a wide range of resources.

resizing
The process of changing the height and width of an object without necessarily maintaining the ratio of height to width.

ribbon
A PowerPoint user interface component that contains task-specific command buttons and menus grouped together under sets of tabs and functional groups.

rotation handle
Component of object borders, which appear when the object is selected, that allows users to rotate objects on slides.

Rulers
Visual reference tools used to accurately position objects on slides.

scaling
The process of changing the height and width of an object while maintaining the ration of height to width.

shapes
Common geometric objects that users can add to presentations.

Sizing Handles
Component of object borders, which appear when the object is selected, that allow users to increase of decrease the size of objects on slides.

slide layouts
Templates that determine the placement of various content types on slides.

slides
Individual presentation objects that are used to display content to the audience.

Slides tab
A PowerPoint user interface component that, by default, appears within the left pane and allows users to access and navigate the slides in a presentation.

slideshow
A presentational feature of PowerPoint that displays slides on screen in a particular sequence.

spacing
The vertical distance between lines of text or paragraphs.

Spell Checker feature
A PowerPoint feature that scans all of the text in a presentation to check for spelling errors.

status bar
A PowerPoint user interface component that appears along the bottom of the PowerPoint window. The status bar contains information about the currently selected slide, and provides the user with access to commands for some of the basic viewing features within PowerPoint.

Switch Row/Column feature
A PowerPoint feature that allows users to change the orientation of data along the X and Y axes of a chart without having to re-enter the data.

tables
Containers for numerical data and other content that are organized into columns and rows of individual cells.

template
An existing presentation that contains content placeholders that are already formatted.

text boxes
Blank containers for adding text to slides in PowerPoint.

text placeholders
Containers for text that display instructional text indicating the type of content users should enter.

themes
A combinations of colors, fonts, and effects that provide a consistent look and feel throughout a presentation.

thesaurus
Research tool that provides users with a list of synonyms and antonyms for a particular word.

transitions
Visual effects that occur as users advance from one slide to the next in a slide show.

WordArt styles
Predetermined formatting configurations that can be applied to the text in a presentation.

Index

Slide Show tab *28*
otation handle *32*
ulers *58*

S

ave As command *15*
ave command *14*
caling objects *84*
creenshot tool *72*
creen tips *5*
electing
    objects *82*
    text *32*
election pane *82*
et Transparent Color option *89*
hape effects options *63*
hapes
    fill options *61*
    outline options *62*
izing handles *32*
lide layouts
    types *39*
lide orientation *39*
lides *2*
lide Show functional group *4*
lide Show view *28*
lide show viewing options *28*
lide Sorter view *27*
lides tab *6*
pacing options *58*
pell checker feature *129*
tatus bar *8*

T

ables
    creation options *102*
    fill options *107*
    inserting into a presentation *103*
    navigation methods *103*
    Table Styles gallery *106*
able Tools contextual tab *105*
emplates *24*
ext alignment *56, 57*
ext boxes
    formatting *61*
ext Direction options *58*
ext placeholders *13*
ext selection techniques *32*
heme components *44*
hemes *43*

thesaurus *131*
transitions *133*
Transitions functional group *4*
Trust bar *29*

V

vertical text alignment *57*
View functional group *4*
View tab *27*

W

WordArt styles *50*